GERMAN
SHEPHERD

• DOG BREED HANDBOOKS •

GERMAN SHEPHERD

DR. BRUCE FOGLE

SPECIAL PHOTOGRAPHY BY
TRACY MORGAN

DORLING KINDERSLEY
LONDON · NEW YORK · STUTTGART · MOSCOW
www.dk.com

A DORLING KINDERSLEY BOOK
www.dk.com
Project Editor JILL FORNARY
Art Editor SARAH GOODWIN
Editor SARAH LILLICRAPP
Designer WENDY BARTLET
Managing Editor FRANCIS RITTER
Managing Art Editor DEREK COOMBES
DTP Designer CRESSIDA JOYCE
Picture Researcher JO CARLILL
Production Controller ADRIAN GATHERCOLE

4 6 8 10 9 7 5 3

First published in Great Britain in 1996
by Dorling Kindersley Limited,
9 Henrietta Street, London WC2E 8PS

A CIP catalogue record for this book is
available from the British Library

ISBN 0 7513 0266 X

Reproduced by Colourscan, Singapore
Printed in Hong Kong by Wing King Tong

CONTENTS

INTRODUCTION

MANY CENTURIES of evolution have produced today's domestic dog breeds from their common wolf ancestor. Over 15,000 years ago, when our ancient relatives first created semi-permanent settlements, local wolves in turn moved into the areas surrounding the encampments to scavenge for food. Only the smallest and tamest of these "self-domesticated" wolves survived, and within a very short time the modified wolf-dog had emerged.

Although the German Shepherd looks similar to its distant relative, the wolf, it exhibits a far more tractable character

The early human settlers, recognizing potential uses for these creatures, began capturing young cubs and raising them to protect their campsites and assist in hunting.

ADAPTATION OF THE BREED

By about 6,000 years ago, selective breeding by humans had produced many different dog breeds with enhanced qualities for specific roles, including guarding, load-bearing, and hunting. The development of agriculture demanded yet another canine ability, to guard and herd livestock. Careful mating of those dogs that excelled at this hard work produced numerous herding breeds throughout Europe, varying in physical characteristics, and it is from this genetic "soup" that the modern German Shepherd eventually emerged – not by chance, but through highly selective breeding. Although today few German Shepherds are used as herders, these refined origins have made them among the most versatile and trainable of all dogs.

Selective breeding has increased the fertility of dogs, yielding larger litters than those of their wolf ancestors

Ever alert and always keen to serve, the German Shepherd is justly renowned for its obedience and loyalty

Its authoritative bark and protective inclination to guard and defend home territory make the German Shepherd an effective security dog

NATURAL PROTECTIVE INSTINCTS

The German Shepherd is not by nature particularly aggressive, ranking average compared with other dog breeds. Yet the Shepherd has been specifically bred not only for supreme responsiveness to command but to retain its instinctive canine disposition to guard and protect. This combination has made it the world's most successful security dog.

THE IDEAL COMPANION

Its adaptability and alertness have made the German Shepherd a favourite service breed – Shepherds were the first guide dogs for the blind, and are now also used in all types of rescue work, the detection of drugs and explosives, and in many other assistance and police roles. The dog's exceptional qualities have even taken it to Hollywood, where Rin Tin Tin was the first internationally famous canine film star. But for many devotees

As its name suggests, the Shepherd has a natural herding instinct, which stems from its original working role

of the breed, the German Shepherd's most outstanding characteristic is its loyal dedication to its owner – making it the perfect companion dog, and surely destined to grow ever more popular world-wide.

Superb responsiveness to training, noble features, and an unsurpassed service record ensure that the German Shepherd is one of the most celebrated and popular of breeds

THE IDEAL CHOICE

THE GERMAN SHEPHERD is indeed an impressive breed – noble and handsome in appearance, highly alert, and always full of life. However, before choosing a Shepherd either for showing or as a pet, make sure that you are the right owner for such an energetic and spirited dog.

LOYAL PROTECTOR OF THE HOME

Most dogs are kept primarily as companions, but even the smallest can also provide security through its vigilance and keen senses. Because of its imposing size, looks, and protective, ever–alert nature, the German Shepherd is virtually ideal as a guard dog, but behaviour must be socially acceptable. Correct training and early interaction with other animals is vital.

DOGS ARE NOT WEAPONS

Pet Shepherds may be trained to bark on command and to guard, but should never be taught to attack. Inappropriate training for aggression denigrates the breed, presenting an unfair image to the general public and potential owners. Because mature German Shepherds can be physically intimidating, their handling carries special responsibilities.

BOUNDING WITH ENERGY

German Shepherds are large dogs which thrive on physical and mental activity. Consider acquiring one only if you can provide it with the space, exercise, and attention it needs. Bored Shepherds lead unhappy lives, and through frustration may tend to be vocal and even destructive. Properly cared for, this vigorous, responsive breed can be among the most rewarding of all dogs to own.

Play is integral part of relationship between dog and owner

"Perfection" or Personality?

While breeders may try to produce show-quality specimens which conform as closely as possible to the official standard set for the breed, individual dogs will deviate in certain ways from the ideal. However, a winning character is certainly the most important quality for a good companion, and idiosyncratic features are often endearing.

Puppy has lopped ear which will probably, but not necessarily, straighten out

An Affable, Obedient Companion

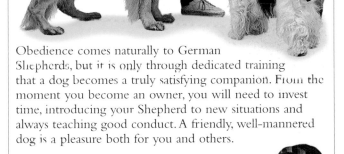

Well-trained Shepherd interacts happily with strangers and other animals

Obedience comes naturally to German Shepherds, but it is only through dedicated training that a dog becomes a truly satisfying companion. From the moment you become an owner, you will need to invest time, introducing your Shepherd to new situations and always teaching good conduct. A friendly, well-mannered dog is a pleasure both for you and others.

Cared for as One of the Family

A dog can provide an enormous amount of companionship and affection, but you must be prepared to care for your pet for at least the next 13 years. Like a young child, it depends on you for its health and well-being. Make sure you can cope with inconveniences such as house training and moulted hair, as well as the expense of food and veterinary attention.

Dog enriches family life, but is totally reliant on you

BREED CHARACTERISTICS

THE BEAUTIFULLY PROPORTIONED German Shepherd has a powerful, supple body reflecting its development as a versatile working dog. Alert, tractable, and steady in character, the Shepherd is dedicated to its master and composed with strangers. A resilient spirit, calm self-confidence, and superb looks are among the qualities that distinguish this fine breed.

WATCHFULLY ATTENTIVE
Good breeding emphasizes a calm, tractable, and trustworthy nature as well as noble looks and physical strength. The keen, alert Shepherd shows great devotion and loyalty.

MUSCULAR AND WELL BALANCED
A slightly long body in relation to height gives the breed a far-reaching, elegant gait. The German Shepherd's powerful yet agile physique and tireless, responsive spirit make it a superbly adaptable working dog as well as a fine, dutiful companion.

BACK
Straight and strong; top line of body is long and flowing, sloping gently downwards towards hindquarters

DOUBLE COAT
Hard, dense, weather-resistant outer coat covers thick, woolly insulating down

TAIL
Bushy and long, hanging in sabre-like curve when at rest and raised when trotting

HINDQUARTERS
Powerful, broad, and well muscled, and angled in proportion to forequarters, producing a balanced gait

FEET
Rounded, with amply cushioned, durable pads; toes well closed and arched, with strong, dark nails

SKULL
In perfect proportion to body, fairly broad between ears, with forehead only moderately domed, and blending into muzzle without too pronounced an indentation

EARS
Medium-sized, broad at base tapering to pointed tips, carried erect

INTERPRETING THE OFFICIAL BREED STANDARD

The written "ideal", or breed standard, describing the German Shepherd's appearance and behaviour, remains virtually identical world-wide, yet the way this standard is interpreted by breeders and judges varies. Certain trends, however, have emerged over time, with Shepherds gradually increasing in size; today, they are considerably larger and with a more sloping top contour than when the standard was first devised. Despite these modifications, the standard has always continued to emphasize a sound temperament and working ability along with physical beauty.

NATURAL BEAUTY AND LIVELY SPIRIT
Erect ears and a well-proportioned muzzle give the head a natural, wolf-like appearance. Masculinity and femininity are clearly defined, with the expression bright and calmly assured.

EYES
Almond-shaped, usually dark, expressing a lively, self-assured nature

MUZZLE
Wedge-shaped and strong, about half total length of skull, with firm lips

FOREQUARTERS
Shoulder blades are long, obliquely set, and laid flat to body; length of forelegs exceeds depth of chest

JAWS AND TEETH
Strongly developed, with upper teeth closely overlapping lower teeth

BODY
Fairly deep chest, with oval ribs never extending below elbows, to allow free movement; belly firm and only slightly drawn up

MEASUREMENTS (BRITISH BREED STANDARD)
Height at withers (see page 77):
FEMALE 55–60 cm (22–24 in)
MALE 60–65 cm (24–26 in)
Weight, in proportion to height:
FEMALE 30–40 kg (66–88 lb)
MALE 34–45 kg (75–99 lb)

1.8 m (6 ft)

BEHAVIOUR PROFILE

EVERY DOG HAS ITS OWN personality, moulded in part by its experiences within the litter, and later with you. Heredity is the other important factor, bringing both positive and negative traits for each breed. Overall, the German Shepherd's devoted, spirited character has made it an enduring favourite.

TRAINABILITY/OBEDIENCE

Shepherds are very responsive to training, and typically show great loyalty and obedience to their owners. Only the Labrador Retriever and the Australian Cattle Dog, breeds also specifically developed to work under human direction, are considered more trainable.

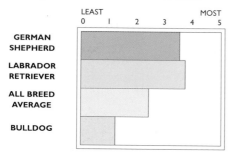

PLAYFULNESS WITH OTHER DOGS

Despite a reputation for mild aloofness with other dogs, German Shepherds are more playful than many breeds, actively enjoying friendly interaction with fellow canines. A lively character and natural inquisitiveness make them in fact a rather sociable breed.

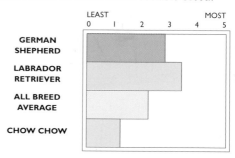

BARKING TO PROTECT THE HOME

The alert Shepherd is an ever-vigilant house guard. While Dachshunds, Lhasa Apsos, and Toy Poodles do just as much protective barking, the Shepherd may also put up a defensive presence. Only the Australian Cattle Dog is less likely to accept intruders.

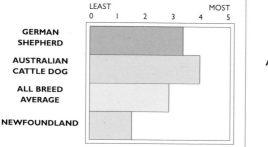

NEED FOR PHYSICAL ACTIVITY

A large, energetic dog bred for work, the Shepherd thrives on physical and mental activity. Only the Australian Kelpie and Cattle Dog and Chesapeake Bay Retriever have a greater need, although early experience influences this trait even more than genetics.

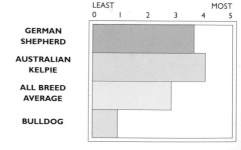

How to Use the Behaviour Charts

In a recent study, experienced vets and dog breeders have assessed over 100 breeds, rating each on a scale of 0–5 for specific personality traits, with 0 representing the lowest score among all dogs and 5 the highest. Here, for eight different behaviours, the German Shepherd is compared with the statistically "average" canine, as well as the breeds reported at both extremes for each characteristic. Note that these findings do not take into consideration either sex or coat colour.

Reliable with Strange Children

German Shepherds are just as dependable with unfamiliar children as the "average" dog, similar to breeds such as the Shih Tzu and Keeshond. Even so, an adult should always be present, and children, until emotionally mature, should never be left alone with any dog.

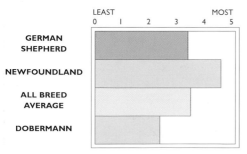

Calm in New Circumstances

In this highly inherited trait, Shepherds are just below average, tending to be slightly nervous or fearful in strange situations, but less so than some smaller breeds. This can be diminished through selective breeding of more relaxed personalities, and gentle training.

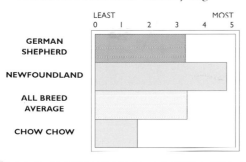

Non-destructive when Alone

Regarding destructiveness when left alone, Shepherds are just below dog "average", about the same as Dachshunds, Schnauzers, and West Highland Terriers. In Shepherds, scratching on walls, digging in carpets or gardens, or barking when alone usually indicate anxiety or worry.

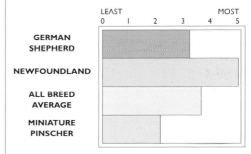

House Trainable

Virtually all dogs respond fairly well to house training, but the German Shepherd and the Labrador Retriever are rated as the most receptive, reflecting both breeds' aptitude for learning, general eagerness to please, and exceptionally willing, dutiful natures.

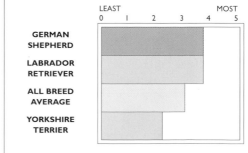

COATS AND COLOURS

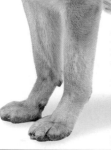

THE TYPICAL GERMAN SHEPHERD is black with tan or gold markings, yet they can also be all black, white, or sable – with black-tipped hairs on tan, gold, grey, or silver. White and long-coated dogs are frowned upon in the show ring. Curiously, coat colour may have a slight bearing on personality.

WIDE-RANGING COLOURATIONS

The developer of the modern German Shepherd, Max von Stephanitz, wrote wisely: "No good dog can be a bad colour." In practice, however, black-and-tan or black-and-gold Shepherds are probably the most popular, with all colours usually preferred to white. Colour-related differences in temperament are minimal; vets and breeders consider all Shepherds to be equally trainable, with no colour more prone to behaviour such as protective or anxious barking, or whining for attention. Black Shepherds are marginally regarded as the most relaxed, affable family companions – slightly more eager to be petted, less destructive when left alone, more playful with other dogs, and less likely to disobey. White Shepherds are generally reported to be the most nervous and disobedient, but the breed's overall character remains outstanding.

SABLE COAT
Black-tipped hairs denote a sable coat.

BLACK-AND-TAN, SHORT COAT
This show champion female's well-defined, rich markings are a fine example of the classic black-and-tan German Shepherd colouration.

SABLE, LONG COAT
Lush, long coats such as this do not meet formal show standards, but their beauty is undeniable.

VARIETIES IN COAT LENGTH

Ninety per cent of German Shepherds are born with standard short coats, and this is the length preferred by breeders. However, the richness and elegance of a long, feathery coat appeals to many Shepherd owners. Some dogs born with long coats have no undercoat, while others produce dense down, offering excellent insulation but requiring more frequent grooming. While a short coat is relatively easy to care for, long coats can become tangled and laden with debris or, in winter, pendulous blankets of snow.

BLACK-AND-GOLD
Deep gold tones give a warm accent to this dog's fluffy coat.

BLACK, LONG COAT
The luxurious coat of this all-black Shepherd features many long, wispy tufts of hair.

BLACK-AND-TAN, LONG COAT
Standard colours are attractively combined with a longer-style coat.

WHITE SHEPHERDS

White Shepherds are disqualified from the show ring in some countries and severely penalized in others. The spurious explanation given is that white working dogs are difficult to see on snow-covered hills, or too easy to spot as night-time guards. Hence, this colour is bypassed by most top breeders and consequently disadvantaged. White Shepherds' unique look, however, gives them widespread popularity as pets.

WHITE, SHORT COAT
The almost pure white colouration makes for a striking appearance.

LONG COAT
Cream shades dominate here.

SEX AND TYPE DIFFERENCES

APART FROM THEIR OBVIOUS physical differences, male and female German Shepherds also vary somewhat in character. Specific "types" bred primarily for working or showing may differ too. Yet all have in common the alert, adaptable nature that has given the breed its well-earned popularity.

PHYSIQUE AND TEMPERAMENT: THE SEXES COMPARED

Male German Shepherds are typically larger and more powerfully built than females, and have less delicate features. Overall, gender also has some influence on personality, with male dogs being frequently more territorial and independently-minded than females.

Head is narrower and smaller than male's

Body is less bulky and lighter, while retaining same proportions

GENTLE, RESPONSIVE FEMALE

Females are often regarded as slightly easier to train than males, and less disobedient. They are also more likely to be playful with other dogs and receptive to strangers, and may want more frequent petting than males. Neutering can sometimes reduce an inclination towards possessiveness.

GENDER-SPECIFIC MEDICAL PROBLEMS

A variety of diseases are caused or influenced by sex hormones. Unless spayed early in life, females of all breeds may suffer from breast cancer and womb infection. Uncastrated males sometimes develop perianal tumours, testicular cancer, or prostate disorders, with associated pain or bleeding on urination. Neutering is part of the preferred treatment for all gender-related medical conditions. Subsequent weight gain is not a major problem with Shepherds.

ASSERTIVE, CONFIDENT MALE

Male Shepherds tend to be more territorial than females, and more wary of strangers, yet are generally not as excitable or as prone to whining for attention. Often more aloof and independent, they can require greater experience to train. Males of all breeds may instinctively try to dominate other male dogs.

Male has larger, heavier body and broader head than female

SHOW OR WORKING TYPE?

BRED FOR BEAUTY

Many Shepherds are bred to conform to the "type" that is favoured in the show ring. Here, "type" is used to describe body proportions – the relationship between length and shoulder height, and muzzle length relative to the skull. Since this may be fluidly interpreted, show Shepherds have evolved over time and continue to vary from country to country.

Successful show dog, trained in formal deportment, adopts presentation stance

Long, flowing top line curves gently downwards to tail

Short coat length is considered correct for show ring

Working dog has been trained to retrieve dumb-bell

Long coat is no disadvantage in an active role

TRAINED TO WORK

Some Shepherds bred for show are also trained to participate in working trials, which require skills in obedience, agility, or scent trailing. However, breeders who specialize in producing working "types" are inclined to select their stock from dogs that have excelled in these abilities. Performance potential is valued over perfect looks.

BREEDING FOR SPECIAL ROLES

German Shepherds destined for specific service duties such as police and security work, or assisting the disabled, are also selectively bred for certain desirable qualities. Sound health and good character are of prime importance, and dogs are screened for freedom from inherited physical disorders such as hip dysplasia and, even more importantly, for an even, calm temperament. In appearance, Shepherds with specialized jobs often depart from the type preferred in top show circles.

FINDING THE RIGHT DOG

HAVING DECIDED THAT you want to acquire a German Shepherd, be selective in your search. Do not act impulsively; seek professional guidance from your local vet or dog training club, and choose carefully according to this advice and your lifestyle. Any purchase should incorporate a veterinary examination.

ADVICE ON WHERE TO BUY AND WHAT TO LOOK FOR

CONSULT A VETERINARIAN

Vets and their staff can provide unbiased information on what to look for in a healthy German Shepherd. They are usually aware of any prevalent medical problems or behavioural idiosyncracies, and their advice is always free of charge.

INQUIRE AT LOCAL DOG TRAINING CLUBS

Contact your local dog training club for sound guidance on how to find a trainable, even-tempered Shepherd. Trainers are often able to recommend specific breeders. While gender and coat colour partly determine a dog's temperament, so do breeding lines.

SUITABLE FOR YOUR LIFESTYLE?

It is important to select a dog that fits into your daily routine both now and as you foresee it in years to come. A German Shepherd is a large, active dog, needing plenty of exercise and mental stimulation. If you are new to the breed, ask other owners about their dogs and try to spend some time with one. If you have a family, acquiring a pet must be a collective decision. Make sure that all family members like the idea, and participate in your search for the right dog.

Pet German Shepherd is established as well-loved member of family

DECIDING ON A PUPPY OR AN ADULT DOG

BUYING A PURE-BRED PUPPY

Although puppies are undoubtedly appealing, they are also very lively and demand lots of attention; be prepared! Reputable breeders, either professional or amateur, are the best source for German Shepherd puppies. Always visit several litters before making your choice, and note the physique and temperament of the mother and, if possible, the father too. Resist the temptation to buy the first puppy that takes your fancy.

Puppies will be ready to leave the litter at about eight weeks

ANIMAL RESCUE CENTRES

Animal shelters always have dogs needing good homes. A rescued Shepherd from a traumatic background is naturally more likely to have behaviour problems, notably anxiety when left alone. Such dogs may take some time to settle into a new home, but can make exceedingly devoted and affectionate companions. An adult dog from a rescue centre could be a sound option if you feel daunted by the prospect of an energetic puppy and want to avoid the inconvenience of house training. However, because unexpected personality quirks can often be difficult to deal with, only experienced dog owners should acquire "recycled" German Shepherds.

HEALTH CHECKS FOR YOUR NEW DOG

Ears are inspected as part of thorough examination

Make any purchase conditional upon your vet's confirmation that the dog is healthy, with no sign of infectious disease, malnutrition, or parasites. Breeders should provide documents verifying that a puppy's parents are free from a variety of hereditary disorders. By law, if a puppy is not healthy at sale, you are entitled to a refund or a replacement.

AVOID PUPPY MILLS

Whenever possible, purchase your dog directly from a breeder. Avoid puppy farms or mills, as they often provide inhumane environments for mothers and give little attention to the puppies' health. Newspaper advertisements can be fronts for mills; be suspicious if when visiting a private home you cannot see the litter's mother. Be wary also of pet shops; some buy from puppy mills and can be fertile environments for a variety of infectious diseases.

YOUR NEW PUPPY

IDEALLY, BUY YOUR GERMAN SHEPHERD puppy from a recommended breeder when it is about eight weeks old. Older puppies and young adults may find it harder adapting to a new home. Make a careful choice after viewing several litters, then get everything ready to help ensure a smooth introduction for all.

CHOOSING THE RIGHT PUPPY

VISITING A LITTER

When viewing a litter, watch how the puppies behave together; some may be retiring, others more bossy. Bear in mind that very assertive puppies often develop into dominant adults and can be more difficult to train, while a shy puppy may grow to be insecure or fearful – a fairly common occurrence in Shepherds. Apart from considering temperament, decide which sex you prefer, then select a puppy that seems bright, alert, and healthy.

Healthy puppy feels firm, and surprisingly heavy

Easy-going puppy is relaxed and content to be handled

THE ONE FOR YOU?

When picking up or holding a very young puppy, always support its hindquarters. If you are new to Shepherds, do not choose the most forward and confident puppy; this one will need experienced handling. Pick the average of the litter, neither too bold nor overly submissive. Ask to see the parents' registration documents, and health certificates verifying that they are free from hereditary conditions common to the breed, such as hip dysplasia.

MEET THE PARENTS

Responsible breeders are proud of their stock and will be delighted to introduce you to the litter's mother and also the father if available. The parents' appearance and behaviour will give some idea of your puppy's mature size and likely temperament. Be cautious with individuals who are unable to show you the mother; they may not be genuine breeders but agents for puppy mills. Reputable breeders will also allow you to return a puppy immediately if your vet feels there is good reason to do so.

SETTLING IN AT HOME

Secure crate allows gentle exposure to new environment

GETTING ACQUAINTED

As soon as you arrive home with your new puppy, introduce it to its own secure "den" – a grilled dog crate lined with soft bedding is ideal. Initially, make the crate inviting by placing food treats or toys inside, and leave the door open. When the door is shut, a resident dog is able to investigate without fear of harassment.

FIRST NIGHT ALONE

The first night that your puppy is away from its brothers and sisters and in new surroundings is always the most difficult. Provide it with a chewable toy for comfort and, if you are willing, place the crate in your bedroom so the puppy is reassured by your presence. Do not respond to plaintive cries, however, or you will unwittingly train your puppy to whine for attention.

Puppy may be restless or anxious at first

SWEET DREAMS

With a little perseverance, your puppy will learn to settle down and sleep. Set your alarm so that you can get up during the night for the first few weeks to take your puppy to relieve itself. Alternatively, line one side of the crate with bedding and the other with paper for soiling. When your puppy is a bit older, it should accept sleeping outside of your bedroom.

EARLY TRAINING

AFTER YOUR PUPPY has settled in to its new home, begin gentle training for obedience and hygiene. Reward good behaviour with praise, stroking, or food treats. Provide toys to keep your puppy alert and occupied, and arrange regular contact with other dogs to ensure proper social development.

LEARNING WITH REWARDS

VERBAL PRAISE

Shepherds are eager pupils and learn quickly. Even a very young puppy will be sensitive to your manner and tone of voice, and will understand when you are genuinely pleased with its behaviour. Enthusiastic words of approval should always accompany any other type of reward.

Touching the head can be seen as a threat; stroke the body instead

Puppy knows it has done well when it hears "Good dog!"

STROKING REWARD

Touch is an intensely powerful reward. Your puppy will naturally want to be stroked, but do not comply on demand. Offer petting in response to good conduct, so that obedience is associated with desired physical attention.

ACQUIRING SOCIAL SKILLS

A puppy's ability to learn is at its greatest during the first three months. If denied ongoing contact with other dogs during this important stage, your German Shepherd may not develop the social skills necessary for meeting strange dogs later in life. If you do not have another dog, ask your vet to help you organize regular supervised "puppy parties" to encourage natural, friendly interaction between healthy puppies of a similar age.

Favourite foods are useful as rewards for good behaviour

FOOD TREAT

Some German Shepherds are so alert to their surroundings that they do not respond immediately to food rewards. Discover which treats your puppy likes best and use these as rewards, along with vigorous praise.

TOYS FOR YOUR NEW PUPPY

Chew toy is excellent for exercising puppy's jaw muscles

SUITABLE TOYS FOR CHEWING AND PLAYING
Well-designed toys help stimulate your puppy physically and mentally. However, Shepherds can be possessive about toys – particularly squeaky ones. Therefore, let your dog see you put all play items away after use, so it understands that they belong to you. Keep only a limited collection of toys, choosing ones that are fun to chase, capture, retrieve, or chew.

TOYS AS REWARD AND COMFORT
While toys left lying around soon become boring, items brought out only under special circumstances are transformed into exciting rewards. When given selectively as a prize for good behaviour, toys can serve as extremely effective training aids. Whenever you leave your Shepherd alone, at any age, be sure to provide it with a well-loved toy as comforting distraction.

HOUSE TRAINING INDOORS AND OUT

PAPER TRAINING
Your puppy will usually want to eliminate after waking, eating, drinking, or exercise. It may signal this by putting its nose down and sniffing. Quickly place the dog in an area covered with newspaper, and praise it when it urinates or messes. It is pointless to punish your puppy after an accident. If you catch it in the act, however, sternly say "No" to teach it that it must use the paper.

MOVING OUTSIDE
Start outdoor training as soon as possible. Three-month-old puppies need to empty their bladders about every three hours. Take a small piece of soiled paper with you; the puppy will smell its own scent, and be encouraged to transfer toileting outside. As it eliminates, say "Hurry up"; this will train your dog to relieve itself on that command.

INTRODUCING OUTDOORS

PUPPIES SHOULD EXPERIENCE the outdoors as soon as possible. Provide essential health vaccinations and identification, and accustom your young Shepherd to a collar and lead. Enlist friends to help you create situations in which the puppy can meet new people and other dogs in controlled circumstances.

IDENTIFICATION

STANDARD NAME TAG
Engraved or canister tags carry vital information about your dog, including a contact telephone number. A dab of nail varnish will stop metal canisters from unscrewing.

MICROCHIP
A tiny transponder, encased in glass, stores important data permanently. Inserted just under the skin on the neck, it can be "read" using a hand-held scanner.

EAR TATTOO
Painless tattoos, bearing a registration number logged with a kennel club or other private organization, provide permanent identification, and are widely popular.

INTRODUCTION TO COLLAR AND LEAD

1 Collar and lead training can begin as soon as you acquire your puppy. Start by letting the dog see and smell the collar. Then, avoiding eye contact, kneel down and put the collar on, distracting the puppy with words. Reward it with treats, physical contact, and praise. Actively play for a while, then take the collar off. Your puppy will quickly learn to associate the collar with rewards, and should accept it without reluctance.

Put on a light, comfortable collar, distracting puppy with words, or using a treat or toy

2 Once your puppy is content wearing its collar, kneel in front and attach a lead. Keeping the lead slack, entice your dog to one side with a toy or food reward. When it moves towards the reward, apply light tension to the lead. Allow the puppy to have the toy or treat, and give it copious praise.

Puppy is rewarded for accepting presence and light tension of lead by gaining access to toy

MEETING STRANGERS

Arrange for a canine-loving friend to meet you and your dog outdoors. Ask your friend to kneel down to greet the puppy, as this will help dissuade it from jumping up. Also discourage direct eye contact, which can provoke a fearful or worried response – not uncommon in Shepherds. Finally, provide your friend with your puppy's favourite food treat to give as a reward for calmness.

Prevent jumping by kneeling rather than leaning over puppy

ESSENTIAL PUPPY INOCULATIONS

Your vet will vaccinate your new puppy against a range of infectious diseases, and for extra protection may advise avoidance of unfamiliar dogs for a few weeks. Contact with known healthy dogs should continue, however, to ensure proper socialization.

ENCOUNTERING OTHER DOGS

Ask a friend with a relaxed dog to meet you on a walk. Have your friend instruct her dog to sit while you walk past, and reward your puppy's calm response with treats and praise. If you have no friends with dogs, you will find that other dog walkers are more than willing to help with this form of training. Through routine meetings, your puppy learns that there is no need to be fearful of other dogs. Regular interaction with puppies of a similar age will also help in developing vital social skills.

Always walk your puppy on a lead for safe control

Well-behaved adult dog sits placidly on command without provoking puppy

Puppy shows interest in strange dog but no anxiety

FIRST ROUTINES

A PUPPY'S EARLY EXPERIENCES set patterns for life. Train your young Shepherd from its first days with you to accept being left alone, to wait patiently in its own crate while you are busy, and to learn about permitted behaviour. Most importantly, train it to enjoy coming to you when called.

ACCEPTING BEING LEFT ALONE

No matter how much you enjoy being with your new puppy, there will be times when you must leave it on its own. Train your young Shepherd to accept that this is part of its routine by confining it to its crate with an interesting reward, such as a hollow toy filled with a little peanut butter. Then quietly walk away, signalling "Wait". Gradually accustom your dog to being left alone for extended periods.

Puppy is content in crate because it has been rewarded with favourite toy

Owner quietly walks away, giving raised hand signal that puppy will soon learn means "Wait"

DISTINGUISHING BETWEEN GOOD AND BAD BEHAVIOUR

Without training, your puppy will simply follow its own natural instincts. Behaviour expectations must be taught, by rewarding good conduct and reprimanding disagreeable actions. Shepherds are very sensitive to tone of voice, and a stern "No!" is powerful admonition. To punish substantial misdemeanours, you may grab the scruff of the neck firmly but without causing pain, mimicking how the puppy's mother would have administered discipline.

SEVERAL PUPPIES?

If you have more than one puppy, train them individually for effective results. It is very difficult, even for highly experienced dog handlers, to maintain the concentration of several lively puppies together!

COMING TO YOU ON COMMAND

1 For safety and responsible control, your puppy must learn always to come to you on command. Use positive training with rewards; never call your puppy to discipline it, or it will then associate returning to you with being reprimanded. Having trained your Shepherd to accept a collar and lead, put these on the dog and kneel a short distance away, with the lead tucked securely under one knee. Hold a chewable or attractively scented toy as a reward; this will be more clearly visible than a food treat.

Appealing toy makes training fun for your dog

Puppies are easily distracted and may ignore you initially

2 Call your puppy's name in a clear, friendly tone to attract its attention. When it turns its head towards you, give the command "Come" and wave the toy as an enticement. Keep the lead slack; do not reel in your puppy but encourage it to come willingly for the reward.

When called, puppy turns and sees toy

Tail held high shows puppy is now alert and eager to obey

3 Welcome your puppy with open arms. Out of curiosity, it should walk towards you. As it moves, say "Good dog" in an enthusiastic voice. When the puppy reaches you, reward it with the toy. Develop a pleasurable bond so your dog comes because it wants to be with you.

COME, SIT, DOWN, STAY

TRAINING YOUR PUPPY to come, sit, lie down, and stay down is most important both for the safety of your dog and for harmonious relations with your family, friends, and outside the home. As a breed, the German Shepherd is exceptionally responsive to basic obedience training.

COME AND SIT

While training, maintain eye contact with your puppy

1 Try to work in a quiet, narrow space such as a hallway, without any distractions. Holding the puppy on a loose lead, cheerfully call its name and let it see that you have a food treat in your hand. As it begins to move, give the command "Come". Be enthusiastic, and while your puppy walks towards you, praise it by saying "Good dog".

2 When your puppy reaches you, move the treat above its head. To keep its eye on the food, the puppy will naturally sit. As it does so, issue the command "Sit" and immediately give the reward. Repeat the exercise regularly until your puppy responds to words alone.

Offer reward calmly to avoid over-excitement

Lead is slack, but can be gently pulled to gain compliance

Tail held out shows puppy is not anxious or frightened

THE UNRESPONSIVE PUPPY

Some German Shepherds are simply not interested in food rewards. While training your puppy, feed it fewer but larger meals to stimulate the appetite. If this fails, try using a favourite squeaky toy as a reward. Puppies can also be easily distracted, so begin basic training in a quiet indoor environment before moving outside, where there are more diversions for a lively and curious dog. Train only for a few minutes at a time twice daily when you, as well as your puppy, are mentally alert. With a strong-willed puppy, use a lead to ensure that it responds.

Puppy stretches along floor to receive food treat

FOLLOW DOWN

1 Kneel beside the seated puppy, holding its collar with one hand, and place a treat by its nose. If your puppy will not sit or tries to get up, tuck its hindquarters under with your free hand and command "Sit".

2 Move the treat forwards and down in an arc, drawing the puppy as it follows the food with its nose. As it starts to lie down, give the command "Down". If the puppy refuses, gently raise its front legs into a begging position, then lower it down, always rewarding obedience with praise.

3 Still holding the collar, continue to move the treat forwards and down until your puppy is lying completely flat. Then reward the puppy with the treat and praise. Do not praise excessively, however, as this can excite your young Shepherd and be counter-productive.

Lead is secured under knee to maintain control

STAY DOWN

Having positioned your puppy down, give the command "Stay". With the lead held loosely in your hand, and maintaining eye contact, get up and walk in front, repeating "Stay". Use a raised palm gesture rather than food rewards; this will become a learned visual signal. Response to the "Stay" command is important in potentially hazardous situations.

Gradually extend length of "Stay" to minutes

WALKING TO HEEL

A MATURE GERMAN SHEPHERD running loose or pulling on its lead can be intimidating to some people, while a mild-mannered Shepherd walking to heel is the perfect advertisement for such a marvellous breed. Some puppies initially train best for heelwork off the lead; others respond well to a lead from the start.

WALKING TO HEEL WITHOUT A LEAD

1 Kneel to the right of your alert, seated puppy. Holding its collar with your left hand, speak its name and show it a food treat in your other hand.

2 Using the scent of the food to attract the puppy, walk in a straight line while giving the command "Heel". Be ready to grasp the collar with your left hand if the puppy wanders. When you stop, command "Wait". Have your dog master the sequence of "Sit", "Heel", and "Wait" before progressing to right and left turns.

Puppy eagerly follows food; or, try a favourite toy

3 Keeping the treat low to prevent jumping up, bend your knees and turn right, drawing the food round as you move. Repeat the command "Heel". Your puppy will speed up to walk round you.

Train puppy to stay close to your leg

4 Left turns are more difficult. Hold the collar with your left hand and give the command "Steady". Place the reward close to your dog's mouth, then move it to the left. The puppy will follow.

Puppy turns to left in pursuit of reward

HEELWORK WITH A LEAD

1 With the puppy on a long training lead and seated to your left, hold the lead and a treat in your right hand, and the slack of the lead in your left. Tell your puppy to sit.

Puppy watches owner intently

Maintain eye contact as puppy waits for next command

2 Move forwards on your left foot while giving the command "Heel". If your puppy strays too far ahead, give the lead a quick, light jerk to pull it back.

3 With the puppy beside you in the heel position, offer it the reward and say "Good dog". Repeat the "Sit" command, and praise your puppy when it obeys.

5 Once the right turn has been learned, commence left-turn training. Hold the treat in front of the puppy's nose to slow it down while speeding up your own circling movement to the left. Keep the puppy close to your left leg and issue the command "Steady" as it follows you round.

4 After the dog has learned to walk to heel in a straight line, teach it to turn to the right by guiding it with the treat. If your puppy has lost interest, break off practice until later.

Puppy slows down while concentrating on food reward

INDOOR TRAINING

ALTHOUGH GERMAN SHEPHERDS love the outdoors, your dog is likely to spend much of its life with you in your home. Make sure that it understands basic "house rules", and provide it with its own personal space to retire to. Give your Shepherd satisfying time and attention, but always on your own terms.

LEARNING TO WAIT PATIENTLY

Your German Shepherd must be made to understand that you are the leader of the pack, and you decide what happens and when. Do not respond to your dog's demands for attention or let it initiate activities. Every dog should have some private space – a bed or a crate that it can call its own. Your Shepherd will learn to retire happily to its "den" while you are relaxing or busy with household chores.

Quilt-type bed is comfortable and large enough for adult dog to stretch out fully

Dog chews toy, not disturbing owner

SPENDING QUALITY TIME TOGETHER

Nurturing the bond between you and your dog is not only enjoyable, but important in reinforcing basic obedience. Set aside time each day to offer your Shepherd some indoor physical and mental activity. Vary the hour and type of play, or your dog will expect a certain game at a given time. Put toys away at the end of play; this makes their next appearance more exciting.

Games keep your dog happy and alert, and are rewarding for both players

UNDERSTANDING WHAT IS WRONG

Use body language as well as words to convey your displeasure

No dog instinctively knows what is permitted and what is not. For example, lying on a comfortable sofa seems perfectly natural to your Shepherd! Unwanted behaviour should be reprimanded immediately so the dog understands exactly what it has done wrong. Be theatrical, adopting an assertive stance and a stern tone of voice, and your dog will quickly learn your intentions.

RELINQUISHING A FORBIDDEN ITEM

Female Shepherds are particularly likely to appropriate appealing objects and take them back to their beds, although males may also smuggle food-scented items like kitchen cloths. Train your dog, using favourite treats, to drop and surrender forbidden articles willingly on command.

ACCEPTING STRANGERS AT HOME

German Shepherds are inclined to bark protectively and "patrol" the home. Some may even try to dominate visitors by jumping up or growling. Train your dog to sit calmly at a distance when guests are present, to discourage territorial guarding. Ask visitors initially to disregard your pet and avoid eye contact; this will help disperse any sense of confrontation. If your Shepherd is vocal, teach it to be quiet on command. Always reward good behaviour with approving words, a gentle stroke, or a favourite treat.

OUTSIDE THE HOME

WHETHER IN YOUR OWN GARDEN or further afield, your German Shepherd must be kept under secure control, both for its own protection and the safety of others. It is important to provide a healthy, hazard-free environment for your pet, and to observe social obligations conscientiously.

SHELTER AND EXERCISE

COMFORTABLE OUTDOOR KENNEL
If you plan to house your dog in a kennel, introduce it from an early age. The kennel should be chew-proof and well-insulated. Make it a cosy sanctuary, but do not keep your dog kennelled alone interminably.

CLEAN, SPACIOUS RUN
A hygienic run attached to the kennel is ideal for several dogs, allowing fresh air and limited exercise. However, Shepherds have large reserves of energy and will still need regular physical activity outside their runs.

CONTROL OUTDOORS

HALF-CHECK COLLAR
Most dogs respond well to a half-check collar. Fit the collar so that the soft webbing lies round your dog's throat, while the chain links sit at the back of its neck. A tug on the lead will tighten the collar, giving firm control without causing discomfort.

HEAD HALTER
A head halter can help with strong-willed dogs. Ensure that it fits comfortably over the muzzle. If your Shepherd lunges, its momentum will gently tighten the nylon halter, pulling the head down and the jaws closed.

MUZZLE
Apply a muzzle either to obey local laws or to prevent your dog from biting. Use a basket variety in the appropriate size and properly adjusted to permit panting and barking. Never leave your muzzled dog unattended for long periods.

USING A FULL CHECK CHAIN

1 To put on a check chain correctly, hold it open in a circle as shown, then slip it round your dog's neck.

2 The chain must tighten only when tension is applied to the lead. If put on backwards, or if the dog is not kept on your left side, the chain will not loosen after tension is released.

ALWAYS GIVE PROMPT DISCIPLINE

German Shepherds are lively, inquisitive dogs that, left unsupervised, may investigate further than you would like. If your dog has engaged in destructive digging, for example, reprimand it at once so that it understands why you are displeased. Enforce a lie down and stop all play; if you are away from home, return immediately. Young male Shepherds in particular may need obedience reinforced when outdoors.

PLANNING A SAFE AND SECURE GARDEN

The greatest hazard presented by your garden is the risk of escape. Check that all fencing is sturdy, gate latches secure, and that hedges have no gaps. Install wire mesh where necessary. Keep all garden chemicals safely locked away, and if you have outdoor lighting, ensure that no cables are exposed and may be chewed. To prevent damage to your lawn, train your dog to use a specific site as its toilet. Be certain to store all waste and any horticultural tools securely out of reach, and do not plant material that may be poisonous to dogs. Always watch your Shepherd carefully near a lit barbecue so it does not lick hot implements, and cover ornamental ponds to avoid accidents.

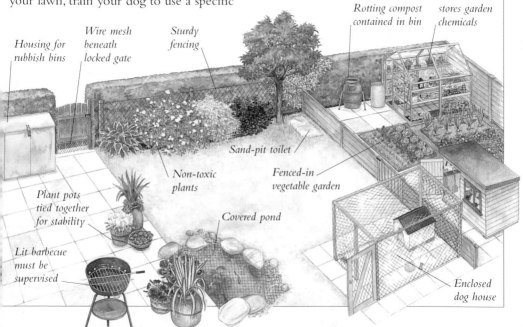

Housing for rubbish bins

Wire mesh beneath locked gate

Sturdy fencing

Rotting compost contained in bin

Greenhouse stores garden chemicals

Sand-pit toilet

Non-toxic plants

Fenced-in vegetable garden

Plant pots tied together for stability

Covered pond

Lit barbecue must be supervised

Enclosed dog house

TRAVEL AND BOARDING

WITH PROPER CARE, your Shepherd should happily accept both routine travel and holidays. Introduce car journeys as early as possible, and make trips safe and enjoyable. Monitor your dog in any new surroundings, and ensure that it will be secure and comfortable if left with others while you are away.

QUALITY BOARDING KENNELS

For holidays without your dog, ask your vet's advice on kennels. Visit recommended establishments and inspect their housing and runs for cleanliness and security. Ask how often your Shepherd will be exercised or played with each day, and satisfy yourself that the staff are responsible. If introduced to kennels early in life, dogs tend to take revisits in their stride. Before kennelling, ensure that your dog's health inoculations are up to date.

DOG-SITTING SERVICES

Especially in urban areas, dog- and house-sitting services are an alternative to kennels. Again, your vet may be able to recommend reliable agencies providing Shepherd-loving carers to look after your home and your dog while you are away. Always leave dog sitters with a list of routine instructions, emergency details, and house rules for your dog.

Shepherd enjoys all the comforts of home with an approved dog sitter

BE CONSIDERATE OF OTHERS

Local dog-control regulations vary. Observe notices, and keep your dog on a lead and under control where obliged. Carry a supply of plastic bags to clean up after your dog, and deposit mess in special waste bins if available. Never let your dog be a nuisance to others.

SAFE TRAVELLING BY CAR

REAR-LOADED CRATE

Professional dog handlers prefer to transport their dogs in crates. These are roomy and secure, and help keep your car free from dog hair or chewing damage. Introduce your Shepherd to its crate during puppyhood, as its regular bed and playpen in the home. Then, when the crate is used as transport, your dog will be inclined to relax and enjoy the journey. On long trips, stop periodically to allow your dog to exercise, drink, and relieve itself.

CANINE SEATBELT

Your Shepherd risks the same injuries that you do in a car accident. Your dog can travel safely on the rear seat of a car using a special canine seatbelt which, like a child's harness, attaches to the standard seatbelt anchors. With this, the dog is kept reassuringly in place and under control, so that it cannot distract the driver. Alternatively, restrict your dog to the back of an estate car fitted with a sturdy, purpose-made dog grille.

DEFENDING TERRITORY

Shepherds are territorial, and a car makes a natural "den" to defend. Your dog's presence is usually enough to deter intruders, but it may still growl or snap at passers-by. If your dog shows such aggression or persistently barks at activity outside, install sunblinds as screening, or sit with it for retraining, admonishing bad behaviour. Remember, never leave your dog car-bound in hot or sunny weather – even with the windows slightly open – or with the heater on in winter, as the Shepherd's typically dark coat makes it particularly susceptible to potentially fatal heatstroke.

CONSTRUCTIVE PLAY

GERMAN SHEPHERDS NEED a great deal of physical exercise, but adequate mental stimulation is equally vital. Create activities that make the most of the breed's resourcefulness and superb trainability. Use playtime to reinforce basic training, to strengthen your bond as owner, and simply to have fun.

RETRIEVE ON COMMAND

Although the German Shepherd is not selectively bred for retrieving, your dog can easily be taught to fetch any item. With praise, train it to hold an object such as a slipper, and then to pick the object up. Progress by teaching the command "Fetch", sending your dog away to retrieve the item, followed by "Come". Ensure a response initially by using a lead, and make sure your dog knows exactly what you want it to retrieve.

"SPEAK" AND "HUSH"

Pre-empt barking problems by training your dog, using food or toy rewards, to "Speak" on command. Once it has mastered barking to order, your Shepherd is ready to learn to be quiet when it hears the word "Hush". This useful "game" helps to enforce household peace while allowing watchdog barking to be turned on and off on your direction.

LEARNED ROUTINES

Physical games are the most exciting for your dog, but even "playing dead" can be enjoyable when rewarded with treats, active play, or praise. This entertaining set piece is an extension of the "Down" command, with your Shepherd learning to lie still until you release it by saying "OK".

Dog obligingly collapses at signal "Bang"

EAGER TO WORK

Satisfy your Shepherd's innate curiosity and desire to serve by giving it something to do. Carrying a newspaper or even a light load of shopping is a pleasant challenge, and your dog will relish the opportunity to assist. Helpful behaviour should always be heartily rewarded.

Giving paw shows dog recognizes your authority

TOYS BELONG TO YOU

When you finish playing, make a point of collecting and putting away all toys. This re-establishes that you are in charge, and playtime is available only through you. It also makes toys more desirable to your dog, and therefore more useful to you as a control tool. Some German Shepherds are possessive, and should be trained to relinquish toys in exchange for treats, lavish praise, or other favourite rewards.

Toy is surrendered for food reward

Store play items in toybox to control game time

GAME OF "HIGH FIVE"

Giving a paw is a submissive gesture. Training your Shepherd to sit and offer its paw helps reinforce that you are the natural leader. When children play "High Five" with the dog, it learns that they too are in command.

THE OWNER ALWAYS WINS

Forget about democracy when playing with your Shepherd. It may see certain games as a challenge rather than simple fun, and must be made to understand that you are always the victor. Avoid activities that are too stimulating, like tug-of-war; your dog might want to win so much that it forgets some of its training.

Ensure that play is still satisfying by finishing all games on a positive note, with food rewards, stroking, or encouraging words.

GOOD CONTROL

LIKE ALL OTHER DOGS, your German Shepherd may present you with behaviour problems. Some Shepherds are sensitive to the unfamiliar; others may be troublesomely curious. Most difficulties can be prevented or overcome through proper care and training, and by establishing positive control.

Dog chews toy contentedly while owner is away

HAPPILY OCCUPIED ALONE

No dog enjoys being left alone, and separation anxiety or boredom can result in destructive behaviour. Always leave and return without a fuss, and exercise and feed your dog before you go out, to encourage rest. Give it a favourite toy, or one with a hollow centre that you have filled with cheese spread or peanut butter.

ACCEPTING UNFAMILIAR SITUATIONS

If your dog is alarmed by a new sight or sound, re-present the stimulus from a distance that does not provoke distress. Reward composure with treats and gentle words. Over several weeks, bring the disturbing object gradually nearer, always rewarding calm acceptance. Your dog will follow your lead, and see that there is no cause for concern.

Dog is wary of child on skateboard

Relaxed, easy-going Labrador is used as the "stooge"

Lead ensures control for first meeting

FRIENDLINESS WITH OTHER DOGS

A well-socialized dog will show curious interest rather than apprehension or hostility when meeting other dogs. If your Shepherd is fearful or aggressive, introduce it to a placid, even-tempered dog. Find a distance where your dog is at ease, and give it a reward. Over time, draw the two dogs closer together. Reward good behaviour on each occasion, teaching your Shepherd not to regard other dogs as a threat.

MEETING STRANGERS

Dog sits politely, accepting presence of stranger

If your Shepherd greets strangers with protective aggression, ask fellow dog-lovers to help in practice meetings. Have them avoid potentially intimidating eye contact with your pet, command your dog to sit, and give rewards when it shows no antagonism. Ask a friend to offer a food treat or toy so your dog learns to welcome approaches from new people. Always stop exercise or games if your Shepherd acts aggressively.

DEALING WITH A WILFUL DOG

Some German Shepherds are more dominant than others and need firm handling. If your dog does not respond to your commands, withdraw all rewards – and that includes your affection! Do not take risks; if you are inexperienced with dogs or concerned about your Shepherd's behaviour, contact your vet or local training club and arrange one-to-one or group obedience lessons. Remember, one ill-mannered Shepherd tarnishes the reputation of the entire breed.

LEARNING TO IGNORE DISTRACTIONS

Owner jerks lead to enforce verbal command "Come"

Even the most obedient Shepherd may lapse when faced with a tantalizing diversion. After training your dog to come on command, create an enticing distraction such as a succulent bone. Recall your dog, using an extendible lead to enforce your command. Trained in this way, your dog will learn to return to you on most, if not all, occasions!

Use extendible lead until dog responds willingly

While investigating bone, dog becomes "deaf" to instruction

RESISTING TEMPTATION

Prevent begging by never giving food while you are eating. Relenting with the occasional titbit will actually encourage this bad behaviour more than regular offerings. If your dog begs, command it to lie down, then look away. When you have finished eating, reward your Shepherd's obedience with play and approving words, not with food treats.

Child avoids eye contact while eating ice-cream

FOODS FOR YOUR DOG

CONSIDERING THEIR SIZE and energy demands, Shepherds can be surprisingly choosy eaters. Fortunately, there is a vast array of commercially-prepared and home-cooked foods to meet both nutritional needs and personal tastes. Remember that you are in control of what your dog eats, not the dog.

CANNED FOODS

Moist, meaty canned foods come in a wide range of flavours and textures to suit your Shepherd's appetite. High in protein, they are usually mixed with dry dog meal to add calories and vital carbohydrates. Canned foods are nutritious and tasty, but will not stay fresh in the bowl for more than a few hours.

Standard variety

Special formula for clinical conditions

"Stew" with gravy

Chunks in jelly

DRY MEAL

Crunchy dry meal is added to canned food to improve the texture, contribute fibre and fat, as well as exercise the jaws.

COMPLETE DRY FOODS

Complete dry foods are well-balanced and convenient to store in bulk. Concentrated, they contain about four times the calories of canned foods, so a dog needs smaller quantities. There are varieties to suit all ages and for specific needs, including medical conditions such as bowel inflammation, to which Shepherds can be susceptible.

HIGH-ENERGY
Puppies require nutrient-rich, easily-digestible foods to sustain growth.

REGULAR
Adult formulas maintain mature dogs on a variety of activity levels.

LOW-CALORIE
Older, overweight, or sedentary dogs need less energy from their food.

TEETH-CLEANING
These large, crunchy chunks promote healthy gums and help control tartar.

SEMI-MOIST FOODS

These foods are packaged in many flavours, including cheese, and have three times the calories of canned foods. A high carbohydrate content makes semi-moist foods unsuitable for diabetic dogs. Like dry foods, they can be left out all day, allowing a picky or elderly Shepherd to nibble at its own pace.

SUITABLE CHEWS

Dogs need hard chews to work their teeth. Avoid small chews that may be swallowed, or bones which can fracture teeth.

Compressed biscuit chew

TREATS AND BISCUITS

Snack foods can be very useful training aids. Discover which treats your dog likes best, and give these as rewards for good behaviour, not on demand. Although obesity is not a serious problem with most Shepherds, limit the amount of high-calorie snacks given daily.

BACON-FLAVOURED

SAVOURY RINGS

MEATY CHUNKS

LIVER ROUNDS

TABLE FOODS

In general, a diet that is well-balanced for us is also nourishing for canines. Never encourage begging by feeding scraps from the table, but prepare a special portion for your dog. White meat with pasta or rice is an excellent meal, but avoid strong spices.

Chicken is easily digested and lower in calories than red meat

When serving, mix rice or pasta with meat to ensure all is eaten

CONVALESCING DIETS

German Shepherds are somewhat prone to gastrointestinal upsets. If your dog is recovering from illness, offer it easily-digested foods such as scrambled eggs or a special diet prescribed by your vet.

Light, fresh-cooked scrambled eggs are ideal for sensitive stomachs

HEALTHY EATING

A NUTRITIOUS DIET and sound eating habits are essential to good health. Provide the right foods in the correct quantity for your dog's needs. Although German Shepherds are not generally as food-orientated as many other breeds, prevent begging or obesity by feeding at set times.

DIETARY NEEDS FOR ALL AGES

Puppy lies down for a relaxing meal

GROWING PUPPY
Puppies need plenty of nutrients for healthy growth. Up to 12 weeks of age, feed your puppy four times daily. Reduce this to three meals until it is six months old, then feed twice a day through to the first year.

Bowl has non-slip bottom for easier eating

FEEDING ROUTINES

It is important to establish a strict routine for mealtimes. Train your dog to sit and wait in the presence of food and to eat only when released to do so. Never offer titbits while you are eating, and always give food in the dog's own bowl. Prevent food guarding in a puppy by touching it occasionally during its meals.

Dog waits patiently for signal to eat

MATURE ADULT
The dietary requirements of an adult dog vary enormously, depending upon its health, activity levels, and temperament. Relaxed, easy-going Shepherds may be prone to weight gain. As a general rule, feed your dog once or twice daily.

ELDERLY SHEPHERD
Older, as well as neutered, dogs have lower energy demands and should be fed smaller portions or less calorie-rich foods. Protein intake may be reduced to help prevent obesity, which places undue strain on the hind legs and organs such as the kidneys.

DAILY ENERGY DEMANDS FOR ALL STAGES OF LIFE

AGE	WEIGHT	CALORIES	DRY FOOD	SEMI-MOIST	CANNED/MEAL
2 MONTHS	4.5 kg (11 lb)	1,005	300 g (11 oz)	335 g (12 oz)	500 g/170 g (18 oz/6 oz)
3 MONTHS	9 kg (20 lb)	1,560	465 g (16 oz)	500 g (18 oz)	780 g/265 g (28 oz/9 oz)
6 MONTHS	22 kg (49 lb)	2,160	645 g (23 oz)	700 g (25 oz)	1080 g/380 g (38 oz/13 oz)
TYPICAL ADULT	22–43 kg (49–95 lb)	1,120–1,850	335–555 g (12–20 oz)	380–630 g (13–22 oz)	555–925 g/190–300 g (20–33 oz/7–11 oz)
ACTIVE ADULT	22–43 kg (49–95 lb)	1,270–2,100	380–630 g (13–22 oz)	425–700 g (15–25 oz)	630–1050 g/215–380 g (22–37 oz/8–13 oz)
VERY ACTIVE ADULT	22–43 kg (49–95 lb)	1,780–2,940	530–880 g (19–31 oz)	595–980 g (21–35 oz)	880–1470 g/300–500 g (31–52 oz/11–18 oz)
ELDERLY (10 YEARS+)	22–43 kg (49–95 lb)	1,020–1,680	300–500 g (11–18 oz)	335–555 g (12–20 oz)	500–840 g/170–285 g (18–30 oz/6–10 oz)

FEEDING REQUIREMENTS

These figures represent an approximate guide only. Remember that each dog has its own specific nutritional needs, and that different brands of food vary in calories.

Always provide a well-balanced diet to meet your dog's energy requirements. If you are uncertain of what is best for your Shepherd, ask your vet for detailed advice.

THE RELUCTANT EATER

Unlike some breeds which will eat almost anything, Shepherds have a tendency to be fussy with food. If you and your vet are happy that your finicky dog is healthy and its meals nutritious and tasty, offer food for an hour and, if left untouched, take it away. Repeat this procedure daily until eating resumes. It may take several days, but hunger will eventually prevail over any pernickety eater! Always provide plenty of fresh water to prevent life-threatening dehydration, particularly if your dog is receiving dry food.

Serve food at room temperature, never straight from the refrigerator

RED MEAT AND AGGRESSIVE BEHAVIOUR

Regular high-protein meals may be related to forms of aggression. An unvarying diet of fresh meat, or cat food, is too rich and will supply more energy than a domestic Shepherd needs, potentially leading to excessively dominant behaviour. If this is a concern, include plenty of carbohydrates and vegetables, or perhaps experiment with meat substitutes such as soya or tofu.

BASIC BODY CARE

GERMAN SHEPHERDS have a fine anatomy and are relatively easy to keep clean. Nevertheless, routine attention is required to keep your dog in good health. Examine its eyes, ears, and mouth daily, and brush the teeth every week. Shepherds' nails also tend to grow quickly and need regular clipping.

ENSURING CLEAR, HEALTHY EYES

Dampen cotton wool with tepid salt water to avoid loose fibres

The eyes should be bright, clear, and free from any discharge, inflammation, or cloudiness. Remove mucus or debris from the area surrounding the eye using a fresh piece of moistened cotton wool. Yellow or green discharge often indicates an infection and requires medical treatment. Also seek veterinary advice if your dog has watery eyes or blinks excessively.

BRUSHING THE TEETH

Check daily for any items lodged in the mouth or between the teeth. Once a week, clean the teeth with a soft brush, working up and down to massage the gums. Avoid human toothpaste, which froths and is swallowed.

PREVENT TOOTH TARTAR

Without routine cleaning, tartar can accumulate on the teeth, leading to bad breath, root infection, and gum disease. In addition to regular professional scaling and polishing, rawhide chews are helpful in controlling tartar build-up. This Shepherd's teeth and gums require medical attention.

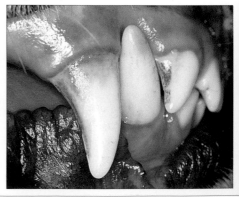

INSPECTING THE EARS

When cleaning the ears, check for wax, inflammation, odour, crusty or scaly deposits, and foreign objects such as grass. Never probe too deeply, as wax can be pushed further in.

Dull pink skin shows no discharge or wax

WASHING THE PAWS

After a country walk, clean your dog's muddy paws in a bowl filled with tepid or cool water. Avoid hot water, especially in cold weather. Rub your fingers between the pads to remove caked, hardened mud. Use a mild soap suitable for human skin, and always rinse and dry the paws thoroughly afterwards.

CUTTING THE NAILS

Command your dog to sit. Use a guillotine clipper rather than a crushing "pliers" type, which would be painful on a Shepherd's thick nails. Cut the tip of the nail, preferably when softened after a bath, taking care to avoid the sensitive quick. Always reward your dog for its good behaviour.

WHERE TO CLIP NAILS
The pink nail bed, or quick, contains blood vessels and nerves, and is hidden by the Shepherd's black outer nail. To avoid cutting into it, ask your vet exactly where to clip.

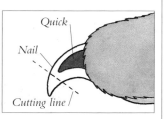

Quick

Nail

Cutting line

ANAL HYGIENE

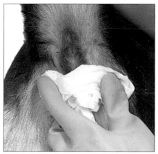

Excessive licking or dragging of the rear can mean that the scent-producing anal sacs are blocked, causing discomfort. Wearing protective gloves, squeeze the sacs empty, applying firm pressure from both sides. Use absorbent material to collect the fluid.

MAINTAINING THE COAT

REGULAR GROOMING IS ESSENTIAL to keep your Shepherd healthy and attractive. Give attention to standard coats at least weekly, and on alternate days during twice-yearly moults. Long coats require daily care while moulting, and from time to time all dogs will have to endure a bath!

ROUTINE GROOMING FOR GERMAN SHEPHERDS

BRUSHING OUT TANGLES
Using a slicer brush, remove dead hair and untangle any mats or knots on the legs, chest, and tail. During moults, much hair will be shed from your Shepherd's woolly undercoat and hard, dense top coat.

"Fingers" of comb reach through coat to massage skin

REMOVING DEBRIS
A bristle brush will rid the coat of debris and loose hairs. If using a double-surfaced brush, apply the pin side gently to avoid damaging the skin. Always check for signs of inflammation, dandruff, or parasites.

Comb through feathering on legs, chest, and tail

MASSAGING THE SKIN
Draw a soft rubber "fingered" grooming device through the coat to stimulate production of natural oils, promoting a glossy, healthy sheen. Alternatively, simply massage with your fingers.

COMBING THE FEATHERS
Particularly on long-coated dogs, comb thoroughly through the feathery hair on the legs, chest, and tail to remove any remaining tangles or stray strands of hair.

Trim hairs between toes

Rub chamois cloth over entire body

Afterwards, reward your dog with praise, active play, or food treats

TIDYING THE PAWS
If the hair has grown long between the toes, trim it with blunt-ended scissors. This will help prevent foreign bodies such as grass seeds from lodging painfully in the paws.

SHINING THE COAT
Complete the grooming routine by smoothing the coat with a clean, dry chamois leather. This wipes any loose flakes of skin from the surface and creates a brilliant shine. Signal that grooming is finished with the release command "OK", then reward your dog's good behaviour with lavish praise.

BATHING YOUR DOG

Keep water and shampoo away from dog's eyes and ears

1 Bathing is necessary after your Shepherd rolls in offensive substances, to treat a variety of skin conditions, or simply to revive the coat's natural lustre. Use a non-slip mat in the bath for safety, and lather thoroughly with dog or baby shampoo and tepid to warm water. Bathe outdoors with a garden hose only in hot weather.

2 Clean the face with a cloth, then rinse off all shampoo, giving special attention under the legs and tail. Talk to your dog in a firm but gentle tone throughout.

3 Squeeze excess water from the coat and wrap your dog in a towel. Let it shake, then rub dry or use a hairdryer set to warm, not hot. Again, finish with words of praise.

ESTABLISH GROOMING AS A BASIC RITUAL

Grooming is comforting to most dogs, but some dominant individuals may resent it. Avoid this by introducing grooming routines as soon as you acquire your dog, as part of standard obedience. It should quickly learn to accept your actions as a sign of leadership. If your dog is strong-willed, command it to lie down and lift its leg to submit to grooming.

BASIC HEALTH

YOUR SHEPHERD DEPENDS on you for its good health. Since it cannot tell you that something is wrong, you must observe how your dog moves and behaves; any changes in activity or regular habits may be warning signs of problems. Arrange annual check-ups, and always use your veterinarian as a source of advice.

EASY, GRACEFUL MOVEMENT

German Shepherds move with a unique elegance, quite unlike any other breed. A healthy dog should walk, trot, and run fluidly and effortlessly. Difficulties lying down or getting up may indicate joint problems – not uncommon, especially in older dogs. Limping is a sign that one leg in particular hurts, and head bobbing while walking usually also means that a dog is in pain. Watch your Shepherd in its daily activities and be alert to any signs of discomfort or obvious loss of mobility.

SOUND APPETITE AND EATING HABITS

Eating and toilet routines adopted during puppyhood are normally maintained throughout life. Even slight changes can be a sign of ill health, and should be referred to your vet. A reduced appetite can simply indicate boredom, but may also signal illness. Asking for food but not eating it can mean tooth pain. So too can sloppy eating – with food being dropped, then picked up and eaten. A heightened appetite without weight gain can indicate a thyroid problem. Increased thirst is always important and may be a sign of infection or conditions such as diabetes and liver or kidney disease. Seek veterinary advice if your dog drinks excessively, or develops chronic diarrhoea or constipation.

Excessive drinking is medically significant

REGULAR PREVENTATIVE CHECKS

Dogs that are vaccinated and have annual health check-ups tend to live longer than those that do not. Many conditions, such as splenic tumours, are not outwardly apparent, but may be diagnosed upon physical examination. Always inform your vet of any observed deviations in behaviour; problems are easiest to treat if detected early. Later in your Shepherd's life, regular twice-yearly clinic visits may be recommended.

ACTIVE AND ALERT?

Canines are creatures of habit. If your dog does not get up when it usually does, moves slower, or is reluctant to play, it could be ill. A stoic Shepherd, however, may try to behave normally to please its owner, even when unwell. Observe your dog closely; if its actions seem even slightly strange, ask your vet's advice.

Using stethoscope, vet listens to heart and lung sounds

Shepherd sits comfortably on table and is content to be examined

MAKING VISITS TO THE VET FUN

Introduce your Shepherd to the veterinary clinic before it needs any treatment, so that it can have an investigative sniff and explore the premises. Ask your vet to give your dog a food treat while it is there, to make the next visit more appealing. Repeat trips can be made less of a hardship for you, too, by taking out insurance cover on your pet's health. This will ensure that you can benefit from the most sophisticated diagnostics and treatments.

CARING FOR THE ELDERLY DOG

Do not expect your dog to remain puppy-like forever. With age, it will slow down and may become hard of hearing, even irritable at times. Be patient with its behaviour, and gentle in your handling. Create less physically demanding activities; older dogs still enjoy playing, but are less agile and energetic. Mental stimulation also helps keep the years at bay.

COMMON PROBLEMS

THE GERMAN SHEPHERD has classic anatomical proportions and a subsequently low incidence of medical problems related to physique. Nevertheless, its lush coat is a superb home for external parasites, while gastrointestinal complaints occur more frequently than in many other popular breeds.

SKIN PARASITES

Fleas are the most common external parasite, although rescued dogs and puppies may contract lice or mites. Ticks are a serious problem in specific areas and seasons.

FLEA INFESTATION
Flea bites cause irritation and scratching. Regularly inspect your dog's coat and use flea-control methods recommended by your vet.

EAR MITE
These microscopic pests burrow into the skin, which becomes very sore and itchy. Clean all bedding and apply special insecticidal shampoo.

OBVIOUS SIGNS OF DISCOMFORT

Check coat for dandruff and visible parasites

Chronic scratching does not always indicate fleas

Paws may also be chewed in response to irritation

SCRATCHING
Dogs often scratch because of parasites, but allergies or injuries can be additional causes. Always have any irritation checked by your vet, who will prescribe treatment, which may include a variety of medications, as well as changes in diet or grooming.

Paw is groomed excessively and may in turn become infected

PERSISTENT LICKING
All dogs lick to groom themselves, but some German Shepherds may do so obsessively, causing skin inflammation and hair loss. Called "lick granuloma" or "lick dermatitis", this exaggerated grooming disorder frequently responds well to anti-anxiety drugs; seek professional advice.

TYPICAL CANINE COMPLAINTS

With any breed, many health problems can be prevented. Routinely examine your dog's skin, ears, and teeth, and keep all essential vaccinations up to date. Apart from the most common ailments, heartworm infestation can be a threat in certain regions; if your area is affected, give your Shepherd preventative medication during the appropriate season.

EAR CANAL

TEETH

INNER EAR

OESOPHAGUS

SPLEEN

KIDNEY

LIVER

STOMACH

INTESTINES

HIP JOINT

EAR DISORDERS
Although the Shepherd's ears are almost ideal, with wide canals and an erect shape allowing good air circulation, infections are not uncommon. Check the ears regularly for wax, odour, discharge, inflammation, and foreign bodies such as grass seeds.

TOOTH CHIPS AND FRACTURES
With large jaws yielding immense crushing power, German Shepherds often delight in chewing through branches and bones. This may be fun for your dog, but to avoid dental damage or mouth lacerations and punctures, try discouraging unsuitable play items.

INTESTINAL PARASITES
Intestinal worms and other internal parasites may cause weight loss, vomiting, or diarrhoea with or without blood and mucus. A dull coat, bloated abdomen, or persistent dragging of the hindquarters can indicate worms. Ask your vet for advice on effective worm prevention.

GASTROINTESTINAL UPSETS
German Shepherds have an above-average incidence of gastrointestinal disorders, and this predisposition is perhaps associated with temperament. However, there are many possible causes of an "irritable bowel"; while diarrhoea can be anxiety-related, it may also reflect a specific food allergy or a variety of other factors. It is best to avoid giving your dog heavy or strongly-spiced meals.

PAINFUL STRAINS
Active breeds such as Shepherds are naturally more prone to muscle, ligament, tendon, and joint injuries. Torn ligaments occur most commonly in the knee, while the hip joint is also easily damaged.

BREED-SPECIFIC PROBLEMS

SELECTIVE BREEDING for desirable traits inevitably also concentrates potentially harmful genes. Because the German Shepherd has been studied so extensively, numerous inherited medical conditions are known to affect the breed. Testing for hereditary disorders, of the bone and blood particularly, can help ensure healthy offspring.

HIP DYSPLASIA

Partly hereditary but also related to obesity or vigorous exercise during puppyhood, this form of hip joint arthritis causes chronic pain and lameness. Veterinary associations and kennel clubs have developed valuable hip-testing schemes for breeding stock.

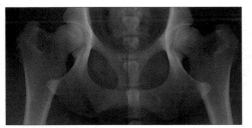 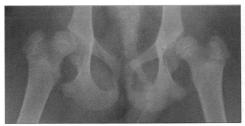

NORMAL HIPS
The hip is a basic ball-and-socket joint. In healthy hips like these, the head of the femur (ball) sits comfortably and securely in the acetabulum (socket) of the hip bone. Dogs screened for hip abnormalities are given ratings, which are listed on certificates that any responsible breeder will hold.

DYSPLASTIC JOINTS
This X-ray of a German Shepherd with severe hip dysplasia shows shallow, rough hip sockets and abrasive femoral heads. Any movement of one against the other causes discomfort. Affected dogs may display thigh muscle wasting, and often "bunny hop" to diminish pain.

CHRONIC DEGENERATIVE RADICULO-MYELOPATHY

More common in German Shepherds than in any other breed, chronic degenerative radiculo-myelopathy usually occurs in dogs over seven years old. Hind leg lameness is the first sign of this disease of the central nervous system, with walking becoming increasingly difficult as partial paralysis develops over a period of months. Although painless, the condition is incurable.

Hind paw not quickly returned to flat position is common symptom of degenerative disorder

OTHER DISORDERS COMMON IN GERMAN SHEPHERDS

Although Shepherds generally have sound, well-proportioned physiques, they are nevertheless susceptible to a number of medical conditions. Some ailments are hereditary and cannot be prevented, but treatment may help to alleviate symptoms.

PITUITARY DWARFISM
A hereditary inefficiency of the pituitary gland results in dwarf German Shepherds. Affected dogs appear normal from birth to eight weeks, then grow slowly, only reaching the size of a small terrier, and eventually becoming virtually hairless.

EXOCRINE PANCREATIC INSUFFICIENCY
In this inherited ailment, the pancreas fails to secrete essential digestive enzymes. Onset is usually before the age of three years, evidenced by a loss of body tone and weight, and the elimination of clay-coloured faeces revealing much undigested food.

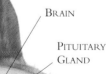

BRAIN

PITUITARY GLAND

PANCREAS

BONE MARROW

SHOULDER JOINT

BLOOD DISEASES
At least five genetic blood disorders are known in Shepherds, where the bone marrow fails to manufacture vital blood-clotting factors. Haemophilia A is a gender-linked condition carried on the "X" chromosome. Von Willebrand's Disease is more common, and may affect up to one in five Shepherds in North America. Clinical severity declines with age.

BONE AND JOINT PROBLEMS
Panosteitis, excessive long bone production, during puppyhood is a breed problem seen largely in North America; this painful condition typically eases with maturity. Osteochondrosis, a joint cartilage abnormality, is increasingly prevalent world-wide. The shoulders and elbows are most frequently afflicted, causing pain-induced lameness. Treatment often involves surgery.

FORESEEING DANGERS

OUR DAILY SURROUNDINGS can present many dangers for a dog. Be mindful of your Shepherd's natural inclinations, and supervise it closely to prevent mishaps. Never leave your dog alone in situations where it may imperil itself or others, and be prepared to avert and react to trouble.

ENSURING SAFETY WITH YOUR GERMAN SHEPHERD

OVERCOMING APPREHENSIVENESS

A fearful German Shepherd may snap defensively, but is more likely to run with worry, possibly putting itself in danger from road traffic. If your Shepherd is apprehensive of other animals, strangers, or unfamiliar noises, reduce its anxiety through remedial training. Be alert to hazards, and use a lead to maintain firm control whenever your dog or others nearby may be at risk.

Nervous Shepherd may bolt out of fear

Outgoing Labrador is seen as threat

CONTROLLING AN INQUISITIVE NATURE

Monitor your Shepherd carefully when off the lead. Adventurous, curious dogs are more prone to injury, and exploratory wanders or investigative digging can result in bites from wild animals, stings, and irritations caused by plants or insects. Keep your dog away from known dangers, and always carry a basic first aid kit to treat minor cuts and lacerations.

DEALING WITH AGGRESSION

Train your Shepherd to be obedient to your command, and avoid situations that may be confrontational. If your dog accidentally or intentionally bites another dog or a person, both you and your pet could face legal redress. You may also be held responsible for property damage. Good training is a social duty as well as sound prevention, but also obtain insurance for your dog's activities.

COMMON POISONS AND CONTAMINANTS

IF INGESTED		ACTION
Slug and snail bait Strychnine rat poison Illegal drugs Aspirin and other painkillers Sedatives and antidepressants	Warfarin rat poison Lead (batteries, etc.) Antifreeze	Examine the package and determine its contents. If the poison was swallowed within the last two hours, induce vomiting by giving crystals of washing soda, a "ball" of wet salt, or 3% hydrogen peroxide by mouth. Consult your vet immediately.
Caustic soda Dishwasher granules Paint remover or thinner Kerosene or petrol Drain, toilet, or oven cleaner	Chlorine bleach Laundry detergents Wood preservatives Polishes	Do not induce vomiting. Give raw egg white, bicarbonate of soda, charcoal powder, or olive oil by mouth. Apply a paste of bicarbonate of soda to any burns in the mouth. Seek urgent medical advice from your veterinarian.

IF IN CONTACT WITH THE COAT	ACTION
Paint Tar Petroleum products Motor oil	Do not apply paint remover or concentrated biological detergents. Wearing protective gloves, rub plenty of liquid paraffin or vegetable oil into the coat. Bathe with warm, soapy water or baby shampoo. Rub in flour to help absorb the poison.
Anything other than paint, tar, petroleum products, and motor oil	Wearing protective gloves, flush the affected area for at least five minutes, using plenty of clean, tepid water. Then bathe the contaminated coat thoroughly with warm, soapy water or mild, non-irritating baby shampoo.

EMERGENCY TREATMENT

With any case of poisoning, look for signs of shock, and give essential first aid as required. Contact your vet or local poison-control centre for specific advice, and begin home treatment as quickly as possible, preferably under professional guidance by telephone.

STORE ALL TOXINS SECURELY

German Shepherds, especially when young, are inveterate chewers. Keep all household, garden, and swimming-pool chemicals stored safely out of reach, and never give your dog an empty container as a toy, or it will regard all similar objects as play items – with potentially tragic results.

PROTECTION FROM ELECTRICAL HAZARDS

Puppies naturally gnaw anything, and often find the texture of electric flex particularly appealing. Train your dog from an early age not to tamper with electrical apparatus, and reduce the risk of burns or electrocution by placing electrical cords out of reach or spraying them with bitter-tasting aerosol. Switch off sockets when not in use and, if possible, add protective covers. If your Shepherd does chew through a live cable, do not risk your own life. Turn off the main electricity supply before administering first aid.

EMERGENCY FIRST AID

A HOME FIRST-AID KIT IS ESSENTIAL for patching up minor injuries.
More serious emergencies are much less common, but
with an understanding of basic principles and
techniques such as artificial respiration and
cardiac massage, you could save your dog's life.

FIRST-AID PRINCIPLES AND BASIC EQUIPMENT

The fundamentals of human
first aid also apply to dogs.
Your objectives are to
preserve life, prevent further
injury, control damage,
minimize pain and distress,
promote healing, and get
your dog safely to a
veterinarian for professional
care. Have a fully-stocked
first-aid kit handy and use it
to treat minor wounds, once
you are certain there are no
more serious, life-threatening
problems to deal with.

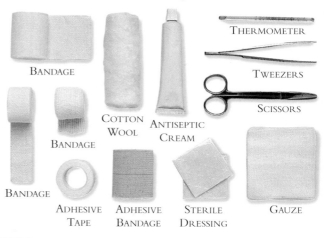

BANDAGE

THERMOMETER

TWEEZERS

SCISSORS

COTTON WOOL

ANTISEPTIC CREAM

BANDAGE

BANDAGE

ADHESIVE TAPE

ADHESIVE BANDAGE

STERILE DRESSING

GAUZE

HOW TO ASSESS AN UNCONSCIOUS DOG

Causes of unconsciousness include choking, electrocution,
near-drowning, poisoning, blood loss, concussion, shock,
fainting, smoke inhalation, diabetes, and heart failure. If you
find your dog apparently unconscious, call its name to see
if it responds. Pinch hard between the toes, while checking
the eyes for blinking. Pull on a limb – does your dog pull
back? Put your hand firmly on its
chest and feel for a heartbeat.
Lift the lip and look at the
colour of the gums. If
they are pink and
when you squeeze the
pinkness out it comes
back immediately, your
dog's heart is beating. If
the gums are pale or
blue, cardiac massage
may be required.

*Pale or blue gums
may indicate life-
threatening shock*

*Shock can either
weaken or elevate
the heart rate*

ARTIFICIAL RESPIRATION AND CARDIAC MASSAGE

Do not attempt to give artificial respiration or heart massage unless your dog is unconscious and will die without your help. If your dog has been pulled from water, suspend it by its hind legs for at least 30 seconds to drain the air passages. If it has been electrocuted, do not touch it until the electricity is turned off. If it has choked, press forcefully over the ribs to dislodge the object. Never put yourself at risk; if possible share first-aid procedures with someone else or have them telephone the nearest veterinarian and arrange transport.

Tongue is pulled fully forwards and debris removed

1 Place your dog on its side, with its head slightly lower than the rest of its body, to send more blood to the brain. Clear the airway by straightening the neck, pulling the tongue forwards, and sweeping the mouth with two fingers to remove any saliva or obstructions. Also ensure that the nose is not clogged with mucus or debris. If you cannot hear the heart, start cardiac massage at once.

Hold muzzle shut and seal your mouth over dog's nostrils

2 Close the mouth, hold the muzzle with both hands, and place your mouth around the nose. Blow in until you see the chest expand, then let the lungs deflate. Repeat this 10–20 times per minute, checking the pulse every 10 seconds to make sure the heart is beating.

Pumping forces blood towards brain

3 If the heart has stopped, begin cardiac massage immediately. Place the heel of one hand on the left side of the chest just behind the elbow, then the heel of your other hand on top. Press vigorously down and forwards to push blood into the brain, pumping 80–100 times per minute. Alternate 20–25 cardiac massages with 10 seconds of mouth-to-nose respiration until the heart beats, then continue resuscitation until breathing starts. A very large Shepherd should be laid on its back and pressed on the breastbone for cardiac massage.

ALWAYS LOOK FOR SHOCK

Shock is a potentially life-endangering condition which occurs when the body's circulation fails. It can be caused by vomiting, diarrhoea, poisons, animal bites, a twisted stomach, bleeding, and many other illnesses or accidents, and onset may not be apparent for several hours. The signs include pale or blue gums, rapid breathing, a faint or quickened pulse, cold extremities, and general weakness. Treating shock takes precedence over other injuries, including fractures. Your priorities are to control any bleeding, maintain body heat, and support vital functions. Unless shock is the result of heatstroke, wrap your dog loosely in a warm blanket, elevate its hindquarters, stabilize breathing and the heart if necessary, and seek urgent medical advice. If your dog begins to panic, try to prevent it from injuring itself further, and take care you are not bitten.

MINOR INJURY AND ILLNESS

EVERY OWNER SHOULD KNOW how to administer medicines and other basic treatment to their dog in the event of accident or illness. Injuries to ears and paws, from fights or sharp objects, are not uncommon, and may require prompt bandaging and precautionary restraint before a vet is called.

EMERGENCY EAR BANDAGE

1 While an assistant soothes and steadies your dog, apply clean, preferably non-stick, absorbent material to the wound. Cut a section from a pair of tights and slip it over your hands. Speak reassuringly as you give first aid, taking care you are not bitten through fright.

Assistant kneels behind, keeping injured dog still

2 With your assistant holding the absorbent pad in place, slip the tights over your dog's head. This pressure bandage will hold the ear firmly, helping the blood to clot.

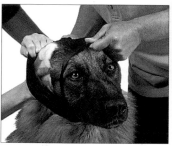

3 If necessary, secure the tights at each end with adhesive tape to prevent your dog from removing the bandage with its paws. The final result provides excellent temporary cover, while also allowing air into the wound. However, you should visit your veterinarian as soon as possible for a thorough examination of the injury.

BANDAGING A WOUNDED PAW

With the aid of an assistant, steady your dog. To control bleeding, apply fresh, non-stick, absorbent material to the cut, wrap the dressing in place with stretchy gauze, and secure it with clinging stretch or adhesive bandage. Do not wrap so tightly that circulation is inhibited, and consult your vet for antibiotics or possible surgery. Change bandages daily to reduce the risk of infection.

IMPROVISING A MUZZLE

Apply a muzzle for safety unless breathing is poor

1 Even the most loving animal is capable of accidentally biting when hurt. With an assistant holding your dog still, make a loop with any soft material such as tights, gauze, or a tie, and slip it over the muzzle.

2 With the loop in place, tighten it gently. Then bring both lengths of material down and cross them under the jaws. If your dog is confused or upset, speak to it in a relaxed, comforting tone.

3 To complete the process, wrap the material round the back of the ears and knot the ends securely. With the muzzle fastened, you can then safely give attention to specific injuries elsewhere.

USING AN ELIZABETHAN COLLAR

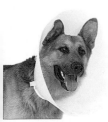

Your veterinarian may provide a lampshade-shaped collar for your convalescent Shepherd, to prevent any scratching or chewing at wounds. This collar should be left on whenever your dog is unattended, but may be removed at mealtimes or during exercise on a lead, when you can deter self-inflicted damage. The device is rather cumbersome and likely to be worn with considerable reluctance!

GIVING A PILL

1 With your dog seated, open its mouth and insert the pill as far back as possible. Liquid medicines may be squirted into the mouth with a syringe.

2 Close your dog's mouth and tilt its head up, stroking the neck to induce swallowing. Alternatively, hide a pill in a piece of meat to simplify the procedure.

ORIGINS OF THE BREED

THE WORLD'S MOST SUCCESSFUL dog-breeding programme began in Germany at the turn of the century, with a dog named Horand, whose noble features and loyal, spirited character inspired his owner to establish a new breed. These same exceptional qualities have since made the German Shepherd a world-wide favourite.

THE FIRST GERMAN SHEPHERD

In 1899, a German cavalry officer, Max von Stephanitz, bought a five-year-old dog called Hektor at a small dog show. Enthused by the dog's fine looks and obedient yet zestful nature, he renamed it Horand von Grafrath and two weeks later, with Artur Meyer, founded the German Shepherd Club, the *Verein für deutsche Schäferhunde*, or SV. Horand, who had a short coat and was roughly 60 cm (24 in) tall – small by today's standards – was the first registered German Shepherd. The SV remains the world's largest breed club.

HORAND VON GRAFRATH

NEAREST RELATIVES

During the late 1800s in southern Belgium, The Netherlands, and northern Germany, there existed a variety of herding and livestock-guarding dogs. While the closely-related Belgian and Dutch Shepherds still have many classifications, German Shepherds were all bred to the SV standard set by Captain von Stephanitz. In this century, the German Shepherd has been used as the basic stock for the development of newer breeds.

GROENENDAEL (BELGIAN)
Long, feathery coat and slim, elongated muzzle

TERVUEREN (BELGIAN)
Almost extinct at end of World War II

MALINOIS (BELGIAN)
Closest in appearance to German Shepherd

SHILOH SHEPHERD
*From 1980s onwards,
selectively bred from
German Shepherds in
United States for good
hips, large size, and
calm disposition*

DUTCH SHEPHERD (LONG-HAIRED)
*Less common than Belgian Shepherd, other
Dutch varieties have short or wiry coats*

**SAARLOOS
WOLFHOUND**
*First developed in
The Netherlands in
1920s by crossing
German Shepherd
with Canadian
timber wolf*

MYTH OF THE "WOLF COUSIN"

The German Shepherd's imposing stature, dark coat
colouring, and striking looks have led some people
to believe that it was developed with the addition of
wolf blood lines. This is not so. The breed evolved
from dogs that are perhaps a thousand generations
distant from their common wolf ancestor. Through
natural selective breeding, the Shepherd's appearance
was gradually altered to resemble that of the wolf.
Experiments in cross-breeding German Shepherds
with wolves have resulted in dogs that
are more nervous, and far less trainable
and responsive than pure-bred
German Shepherds.

CZECH WOLFDOG
*Since 1950s, bred in
former Czechoslovakia
as cross of German
Shepherd and local
Carpathian wolf*

REPRODUCTION

PRODUCING A LITTER of German Shepherd puppies is in itself easy, since both male and female Shepherds are naturally good breeders. However, the decision to mate your dog must be made responsibly – with professional guidance, and the best interest of the breed at heart.

THE MATING INSTINCT

Healthy males as young as 10 months can be used for mating. It is best to wait until a female is about two years old, in roughly her third oestrous cycle, when she is emotionally prepared for a litter. Ovulation usually occurs 10-12 days after the first sign of bleeding and vulvar swelling. The most successful matings generally take place on the male's home turf.

PREGNANCY DIAGNOSIS

Ovulation, the optimum time to mate, is accurately indicated by an increased level of the hormone progesterone in the blood. Pregnancy, however, cannot be confirmed by blood or urine tests. Ultrasound at three weeks or a physical examination slightly later remain the best means of diagnosis.

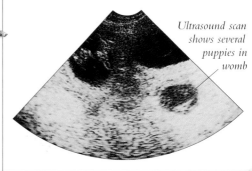

Ultrasound scan shows several puppies in womb

DEALING WITH MISMATING

Mismatings can be avoided by keeping a watchful eye on your bitch when in season, by using tablets or injections to prevent ovulation, or by spaying. If an unwanted mating does occur, contact your vet. A pregnancy can be terminated, usually within three days of mating, with a hormone injection. This will induce an immediate repeat season, demanding renewed vigilance for 8–15 days after the beginning of vaginal discharge.

SPECIAL NEEDS OF AN EXPECTANT BITCH

During the first month of pregnancy, a bitch should continue to exercise freely. Thereafter, the increasing weight of the litter will naturally make her slower and less agile. After the sixth week, food intake should be gradually increased so that by the expected delivery date, the bitch will be eating 30 per cent more than normal. Provide a proper balance of calcium and phosphorus in the diet to promote strong bone growth.

MALE AND FEMALE REPRODUCTIVE SYSTEMS

A bitch comes into season twice yearly, is fertile for three days during each cycle, and will be receptive to mating only during these periods. Males, however, willingly mate year round. For the female, ovulation continues throughout life and there is no menopause, although breeding in later years is risky. Pregnancy lasts for about 63 days.

RESPONSIBLE BREEDING

If planning to breed from your Shepherd, seek professional advice from your vet or from an experienced and reputable breeder. Ensure that the prospective parents' physical and emotional attributes will enhance the breed. Both partners should be screened for certain inherited diseases such as hip dysplasia, detected by X-ray. Your vet may also advise testing for brucellosis, a canine venereal disease. Remember that it is unfair to bring a litter of puppies into the world that will be unwanted or unwell; it is up to you to find each offspring a safe home.

PREVENTING PREGNANCY

Neutering is the most effective and safest means of preventing pregnancy. The female, because she carries the young, is the usual candidate. Both the ovaries and the uterus are removed, followed by a week's rest. The procedure for males is less complicated, involving a small incision to the scrotum for removal of the testicles.

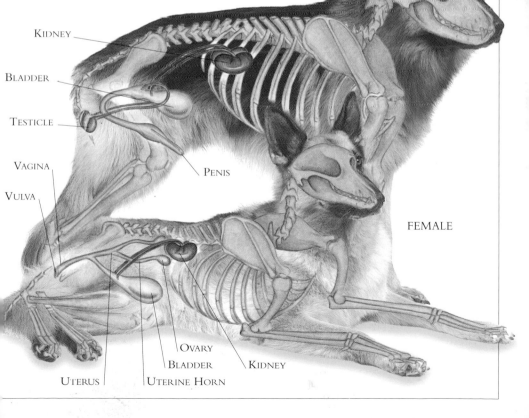

MALE

KIDNEY

BLADDER

TESTICLE

VAGINA

VULVA

PENIS

FEMALE

OVARY

BLADDER

KIDNEY

UTERUS

UTERINE HORN

PRE- AND POST-WHELPING

AS THE DAY OF BIRTH approaches, introduce the expectant mother to her whelping box and arrange for your vet to be on call in case of problems. Although Shepherds seldom have difficulties, it is best to have experienced help both at the delivery and later, for after-care of weak puppies.

INTRODUCING A WHELPING BOX

Several weeks before she is due to deliver, familiarize the mother-to-be with her whelping box. The box should have a length and width of at least 1.2 m (4 ft), and be made of marine ply, which will not be damaged by birth fluids. Three sides should be 45–50 cm (18–20 in) high to prevent the puppies from wandering off, while the fourth should have a lockable opening to allow the mother easy access. Start collecting newspaper; you will need several bundles to line the box and to serve as bedding for the new puppies for the next two months.

Expectant mother feels secure in her purpose-made whelping "den"

DELIVERY CARE

If you have never been present at a birth, ask an experienced dog breeder to attend, and inform your vet when labour begins. Keep the room temperature at around 25° C (77° F). If after two hours your bitch does not produce a puppy, contact your vet once again for advice. The puppy's position may need manipulating to facilitate delivery. Although uncommon, some Shepherds do require a Caesarean section. Place a warm, towel-covered hot-water bottle in a cardboard box, and keep this nearby as a safe receptacle for each newly-delivered puppy. The box may also be used to carry the puppies if mother and litter need to be taken to the vet.

SIGNS OF IMPENDING BIRTH

Your bitch is likely to refuse food shortly before she goes into labour. She will restlessly seek out her whelping box and start to tear up the bedding, preparing a nest for her puppies. Her body temperature will drop, and she may pant. When her waters break and contractions begin, birth is imminent. Avoid distractions and keep other animals and strangers away while the bitch is in labour.

THE NEW LITTER

Young puppies suckle greedily

Towel-dry each puppy after it is delivered and clear its nose of mucus; all newborns should squeal and wriggle. During whelping, offer the mother warm milk. Let her rest after labour has ended and all placentas have been delivered. Place each puppy by a teat to suckle. The bitch will also need plenty of food in the coming weeks – at peak lactation, up to four times her normal intake.

ASSISTING A WEAK OR ABANDONED PUPPY

HELPING TO SUCKLE

On average, one out of seven puppies is born relatively small and weak. Runts are often the least healthy of the litter, and if left to nature frequently die within a few days. To aid survival, place a frail puppy near the teats offering the best supply of milk.

BOTTLE FEEDING

In large, healthy litters where there simply is not enough milk to feed all the puppies, or when the mother is incapacitated or abandons her offspring, use canine milk formula as a supplement. Bottle feed initially every two to three hours, seeking your vet's guidance on the correct quantities.

BRINGING UP THE BROOD

Puppies rely on mother for first three weeks of life

From three weeks of age, the maturing puppies begin to explore; by 12 weeks, the senses are fully developed. Handle and groom all puppies frequently, so they learn to accept being touched by humans, but be careful not to upset the mother, who will be protective. Gentle exposure to new sights and sounds during this early period will help the puppies to grow into well-adjusted, adaptable adults.

Puppies crawl from birth

PREPARING FOR A SHOW

TAKING PART IN a dog show can be great fun, but both you and your Shepherd should be fully prepared. Teach your dog show manners, and make sure it is in prime condition, as it will be judged against a breed standard of ideal physical and personality characteristics typifying the "perfect" specimen.

BASIC EQUIPMENT FOR YOU AND YOUR DOG

FOR HANDLING AND SECURITY

You will need a non-check show collar that permits the judge to have an unimpeded view of your dog's neck, and a slim lead about 1.5 m (5 ft) long. If attending a "benched" event, take a benching chain to secure your dog in its allotted space, as well as an identification number clip.

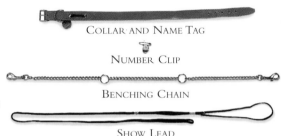

COLLAR AND NAME TAG

NUMBER CLIP

BENCHING CHAIN

SHOW LEAD

TRANSPORT AND SUPPLIES

Your dog will travel best in a crate loaded in the back of a car. Pack food and water for your dog, along with its bowls. If you plan to picnic, also take refreshments for yourself. Folding chairs and a large umbrella for sun or rain protection are essential, as are plastic bags or a "poop scoop" to clear up your dog's mess. A towel is useful for cleaning muddy paws. Keep all supplies, including grooming equipment, in a designated bag for show use.

MEETING SHOW STANDARDS

Visit shows alone first to see exactly what occurs. While working trials require dogs well-trained in obedience and a variety of specialized skills, kennel club events demand only beauty and personality. For these, your dog's coat must be in good condition, its ears clear of wax, and the teeth tartar-free. Bathe your dog and clip its nails a few days before a show, to allow renewal of the coat's gloss by natural oils. No cosmetic aids to improve a dog's appearance are permitted at shows.

Soft chamois mitt is used to shine coat

TRAINING AND TEMPERAMENT FOR THE RING

ADOPTING A CORRECT STANCE
Seek advice from a professional breeder on training your dog to stand correctly in the show ring. This is one of the curious rituals of formal exhibition. Judges respond best to dogs that are placed in and stay in the show position, which allows the top line, hind legs, and head of your Shepherd to be thoroughly inspected and assessed.

Shepherd's head is held high

Hind legs are placed in order that both are visible in profile

ACCEPTING CLOSE EXAMINATION
A successful show dog has been trained from puppyhood to accept being scrutinized by strangers. Reward your dog for permitting unfamiliar people to handle it as a judge would – allowing the hindquarters to be touched, and the mouth to be opened and the teeth examined. Judges invariably prefer dogs that are amenable as well as handsome.

EXCITEMENT OF PARTICIPATING

A dog show is exciting for owners because of the hope of winning, and exciting for canines because it is an opportunity to meet many other dogs. Without early and continued training, some dogs become over-eager and are more intent on interacting with other dogs than on performing in the ring. Train your German Shepherd to be relaxed in the presence of other dogs, and calm and reassure it before entering the ring.

COSTS OF SHOWING

Showing your German Shepherd can be inexpensive, or surprisingly costly. If you show your own dog, your only expenses are entry fees, transport, and accommodation. At higher levels on the show circuit, professional handlers are frequently employed. This can add a very considerable financial burden, and it is a rare dog that is so successful that handling costs are earned back in stud fees or puppy prices. If you are not interested in serious exhibiting, a more sensible approach to showing your Shepherd is to consider it a pleasurable pastime for both you and your dog.

WHAT HAPPENS AT A SHOW

EXHIBITING EVENTS RANGE from informal local competitions, to open shows for all breeds, to exclusive Shepherd championships. Each has its own rules, but all follow similar principles in the quest to find a truly outstanding dog. Shows can provide a very sociable and rewarding day out for owners and canines alike.

SETTLING IN AT THE BENCHES

At some shows, dogs are housed at numbered "benches". Secure your dog with a benching chain and offer it a drink of water. Have someone stay at the bench so your dog does not become bored, and postpone meals until after it is shown to keep it active and alert.

Last-minute combing takes care of any disarray

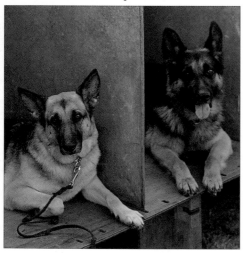

GROOMING FOR THE RING

Just before entering the show ring, give your dog a final groom so that it looks its absolute best; this can also be calming for both of you. It is wise to take your dog to relieve itself too.

Owner gently holds dog while it is being examined

STANDING FOR INSPECTION

When called, enter the ring and set your dog in its "show stance". The judge will examine the body in detail to see how closely it conforms to the breed standard. During the inspection, interfere as little as possible, but keep the head held high for proper presentation. Your dog's temperament is being noted too, and any nervousness, resistance, or aggression will be viewed unfavourably.

RELAXING IN THE EXCITEMENT

Shows are competitive, but many owners view them as an enjoyable hobby offering the chance to socialize with like-minded people and to have a pleasant outing with their dogs.

ASSESSMENT OF THE GAIT

The judge will ask for each dog to be walked round the ring, to appraise its movement. Dogs should "gait" with confidence and fluid grace; a stilted or hesitant manner will be penalized. Symmetry between dog and handler is also important. Some Shepherds are natural show-offs and relish parading in the limelight, while others find it all rather boring.

Legs should flow effortlessly beneath a firm back

BEST OF BREED

Winning dogs have the physical attributes of a champion along with a "star" personality. It is a great achievement if your Shepherd has captured a prize. Yet ideal looks and show style are not the sole criteria of an outstanding dog; any Shepherd in glowing health and with a fine temperament is just as much a winner.

LINE-UP OF FINALISTS

After the individual assessments, a short list of five or six dogs is chosen and inspected once again. The judge will then place the finalists in order of merit, awarding rosettes for first, second, and third place, as well as for "reserve" and "highly commended" contenders.

SPECIALIZED TRAINING

THE GERMAN SHEPHERD is among the most versatile and successful of all breeds – obedient, agile, and exceptionally responsive to command. Shepherds can be trained to high standards to excel in competitive working trials, while their courageous, protective nature also makes them a popular security and police dog.

POLICE AND SECURITY DUTIES

PATROL AND DEFENCE ROLES

Many breeds have been used by both private and public organizations as security dogs, yet the dependable German Shepherd has usually emerged the favourite. At one time, Shepherds were trained by inflicting pain. Today, most professional security forces use less aggressive methods, producing more steady but equally effective guard dogs. Barking at unexpected noises or strangers is central to training.

ASSISTANT OFFICER ON THE BEAT

The Shepherd's watchful, loyal nature and supreme responsiveness to command make it ideal for police work, where dog and handler operate on a system of mutual trust. Some canine "cops" have even been equipped for duty with video cameras so that the handler sees exactly what the dog sees. Usually, police dogs are taught to retrieve rather than attack; training begins with fetching a padded wooden "arm" and finishes with retrieving a "villain" by the arm. A Shepherd trained in this manner is completely reliable, and can be petted by children on a crowded street one minute, and chase and capture a culprit the next.

ADVANCED OBEDIENCE TRIALS

RETRIEVING A DUMB-BELL
Competitive obedience trials provide good mental stimulation. Begin classes at six months, after your dog has mastered walking on a lead and basic commands. Advanced training includes close and fast-pace heelwork, retrieves, recalls, distant control, sustained sit/downs (at times with the handler out of sight), and scent discrimination.

SEND-AWAY COMMAND
A higher-level obedience skill is the "send-away", where a dog is sent into a square area, commanded to turn and lie down facing its owner, then to return. Dogs also learn to stay down unattended for as long as 10 minutes.

TRAINING IN AGILITY

CLIMBING A LADDER
Agility courses open to all dogs are run "against the clock". Although the German Shepherd is not as fast as some other breeds, it is very nimble and performs with the best. Climbing a ladder is a sophisticated test of agility used only in police dog-training programmes.

JUMPING HURDLES
Agility work requires dexterity, confidence, and instant response to command, and can be an excellent channel for restless energy. Standard trial apparatus includes an "A" frame, hurdles, a tyre, poles to weave through, a tunnel, and a see-saw. Training demands ample patience; start when your dog is a year old by enrolling in a local club.

ASSISTANCE ROLES

ALTHOUGH A RELATIVELY new breed – developed this century – the German Shepherd already has a magnificent record of service. From initial work in the fields of war, these able dogs have been employed for police and security duties, to assist the disabled, and in scent trailing for search and rescue or detection roles.

A DISTINGUISHED HISTORY OF SERVICE

In the early 1900s the German Shepherd's role was as a farm worker, but World War I created new needs which the adaptable Shepherd aptly filled. It served as a Red Cross dog searching for wounded soldiers and carrying first-aid equipment, and was a battlefield messenger, telephone cable layer, sentry, and defender of ammunition dumps. At the end of the war, British and American army personnel took Shepherds home. Because it was known as a German dog, British breeders changed the name to Alsatian Wolf Dog, and then simply Alsatian. The Shepherd expanded its services under that name, which survived until the 1970s.

FIRST GUIDE DOGS

Following World War I, the German government trained Shepherds to act as eyes for blinded soldiers. Guide-dog training was furthered in Switzerland and from there, in the 1930s, the concept was exported to France, Britain, and North America. Pictured here is Buddy III, among the first official guide dogs brought to the United States from Switzerland. By the 1950s the Shepherd was the world's most popular dog for assisting the blind. In many countries it remains the guide-dog breed of choice.

TRAINED FOR ASSISTANCE WORK

German Shepherds are selectively bred for good health and the necessary temperament for guide-dog work. Initial training during puppyhood is often conducted in the homes of volunteers. Formal instruction then follows at a specialized training centre, where the dog is taught to see and think for its blind owner, warning of obstacles or dangers. Owners also receive training to understand their individual guide dog.

SEARCH AND RESCUE ROLES

In earthquakes and avalanches, search and rescue Shepherds trained to follow ground and air scent trails perform superbly. Many also work in mountainous regions, locating people lost in fog or unknown terrain. The dogs draw attention to humans buried in snow or debris by digging or barking.

IDEAL POLICE PARTNER

Police and security forces employ the Shepherd as a multi-purpose worker – in search and rescue, scent trailing, defence, and some forms of attack. Each dog and handler operate as a team. Ideally, the handler acquires his dog as a puppy and raises it with his own family, teaching it basic obedience with the help of the police training school. Once the dog is fully mature, the team enters full-time training at the school. Training and assessment continue throughout the dog's working career. Dogs often finally retire to their handlers' homes.

SCENT TRAILING

Government and other agencies often use German Shepherds to detect contraband, illicit drugs, explosives, and other prohibited items at borders, airports, and harbours, working both on open land and in buildings.

BREED STANDARD

A BREED STANDARD is used by the governing kennel club of each country to describe the ideal German Shepherd. Show dogs are judged against this formal index of the unique physical qualities, demeanour, and personality traits that characterize a "perfect" specimen of the breed.

GERMAN SHEPHERD DOG
WORKING GROUP
(Last revised March 1994)

Reproduced by kind permission of
The Kennel Club
London, England

GENERAL APPEARANCE Slightly long in comparison to height; of powerful, well muscled build with weather-resistant coat. Relation between height, length, position and structure of fore and hindquarters (angulation) producing far-reaching, enduring gait. Clear definition of masculinity and femininity essential, and working ability never sacrificed for mere beauty.

CHARACTERISTICS Versatile working dog, balanced and free from exaggeration. Attentive, alert, resilient and tireless with keen scenting ability.

TEMPERAMENT Steady of nerve, loyal, self-assured, courageous and tractable. Never nervous, over-aggressive or shy.

HEAD AND SKULL Proportionate in size to body, never coarse, too fine or long. Clean cut; fairly broad between ears. Forehead slightly domed; little or no trace of central furrow. Cheeks forming softly rounded curve, never protruding. Skull from ears to bridge of nose tapering gradually and evenly, blending without too pronounced stop into wedge-shaped powerful muzzle. Skull approximately 50 per cent of overall length of head. Width of skull corresponding approximately to length, in males slightly greater, in females slightly less. Muzzle strong, lips firm, clean and closing tightly. Top of muzzle straight, almost parallel to forehead. Short, blunt, weak, pointed, overlong muzzle undesirable.

EYES Medium-sized, almond-shaped, never protruding. Dark brown preferred, lighter shade permissible, provided expression good and general harmony of head not destroyed. Expression lively, intelligent and self-assured.

EARS Medium-sized, firm in texture, broad at base, set high, carried erect, almost parallel, never pulled inwards or tipped, tapering to a point, open at front. Never hanging. Folding back during movement permissible.

MOUTH Jaws strongly developed. With a perfect, regular and complete scissors bite, i.e. upper teeth closely overlapping lower teeth and set square to the jaws. Teeth healthy and strong. Full dentition desirable.

NECK Fairly long, strong, with well developed muscles, free from throatiness. Carried at 45 degrees angle to horizontal, raised when excited, lowered at fast trot.

FOREQUARTERS Shoulder blades long, set obliquely (45 degrees) laid flat to body. Upper arm strong, well muscled, joining shoulder blade at approximately 90 degrees. Forelegs straight from pasterns to elbows viewed from any angle, bone oval rather than round. Pasterns firm, supple and slightly angulated. Elbows neither tucked in nor turned out. Length of foreleg exceeding depth of chest.

BODY Length measured from point of breast bone to rear edge of pelvis, exceeding height at withers. Correct ratio 10 to 9 or 8 and a half. Undersized dogs, stunted growth, high-legged dogs, those too heavy or too light in build, over-loaded fronts, too short overall appearance, any feature detracting from reach or endurance of gait, undesirable. Chest deep (45–48 per cent) of height at shoulder, not too broad, brisket long, well developed. Ribs well formed and long; neither barrel-shaped nor too flat; allowing free movement of elbows when gaiting. Relatively short loin. Belly firm, only slightly drawn up. Back between withers and croup, straight, strongly developed, not too long. Overall length achieved by correct angle of well laid shoulders, correct length of croup and hindquarters. Withers long, of good height and well defined, joining back in a smooth line without disrupting flowing topline, slightly sloping from front to back. Weak, soft and roach backs undesirable and should be rejected. Loin broad, strong, well muscled. Croup long, gently curving downwards to tail without disrupting flowing topline. Short, steep or flat croups undesirable.

HINDQUARTERS Overall strong, broad and well muscled, enabling effortless forward propulsion of whole body. Upper thighbone, viewed from side, sloping to slightly longer lower thighbone. Hind angulation sufficient if imaginary line dropped from point of buttocks cuts through lower thigh just in front of hock, continuing down slightly in front of hindfeet. Angulations corresponding approximately with front angulation, without over-angulation, hock strong. Any tendency towards over-angulation of hindquarters reduces firmness and endurance.

FEET Rounded toes well closed and arched. Pads well cushioned and durable. Nails short, strong and dark in colour. Dewclaws removed from hindlegs.

TAIL Bushy-haired, reaches at least to hock – ideal length reaching to middle of metatarsus. At rest tail hangs in slight sabre-like curve; when moving raised and curve increased, ideally never above level of back. Short, rolled, curled, generally carried badly or stumpy from birth, undesirable.

GAIT/MOVEMENT Sequence of step follows diagonal pattern, moving foreleg and opposite hindleg forward simultaneously; hindfoot thrust forward to midpoint of body and having equally long reach with forefeet without any noticeable change in backline.

COAT Outer coat consisting of straight, hard, close-lying hair as dense as possible; thick undercoat. Hair on head, ears, front of legs, paws and toes short; on back, longer and thicker; in some males forming slight ruff. Hair longer on back of legs as far down as pasterns and stifles and forming fairly thick trousers on hindquarters. No hard and fast rule for length of hair; mole-type coats undesirable.

COLOUR Black or black saddle with tan, or gold to light grey markings. All black, all grey, with lighter or brown markings referred to as Sables. Nose black. Light markings on chest or very pale colour on inside of legs permissible but undesirable, as are whitish nails, red-tipped tails or wishy-washy faded colours defined as lacking in pigmentation. Blues, livers, albinos, whites (i.e. almost pure white dogs with black noses) and near whites *highly undesirable*. Undercoat, except in all black dogs, usually grey or fawn. Colour in itself is of secondary importance having no effect on character or fitness for work. Final colour of a young dog only ascertained when outer coat has developed.

SIZE Ideal height (from withers and just touching elbows): dogs: 62.5 cms (25 ins); bitches: 57.5 cms (23 ins). 2.5 cms (1 ins) either above or below ideal permissible.

FAULTS Any departure from the foregoing points should be considered a fault and the seriousness with which the fault should be regarded should be in exact proportion to its degree.

NOTE Male animals should have two apparently normal testicles fully descended into the scrotum.

GLOSSARY

ANGULATION The angles formed at a joint by the meeting of the bones.

BRISKET The forepart of the body below the chest between forelegs.

CROUP (RUMP) The part of the back from the front of the pelvis to root of the tail.

DEWCLAW Fifth digit on the inside of the legs.

DOMED Evenly rounded in skull; convex instead of flat.

GAIT The pattern of footsteps at various rates of speed, each pattern distinguished by a particular rhythm and footfall.

HOCK The tarsus or collection of bones of the hind leg forming the joint between the second thigh and the metatarsus.

LOIN Region of the body on either side of vertebral column between the last ribs and the hindquarters.

METATARSALS Bones between the hock joint and foot.

MUZZLE The head in front of the eyes, nasal bone, nostrils, and jaws; foreface.

PASTERN The region of the foreleg between the carpus or wrist and the digits.

ROACH BACK A convex curvature of the back towards the loin.

STIFLE The joint of the hind leg between the thigh and the second thigh; the dog's knee.

STOP The step up from muzzle to skull; indentation between the eyes where the nasal bone and skull meet.

WITHERS The highest point of the body, immediately behind the neck.

WORKING DOG A dog originally used for work such as herding and guarding.

INDEX

ACKNOWLEDGMENTS

AUTHOR'S ACKNOWLEDGMENTS

Many thanks to all those who were involved in the production of this handbook, with particular gratitude to Patricia Holden White for choreographing several photographic sessions, the Murkett family for lending me their excellent library of vintage German Shepherd books, Gary Clayton Jones for supplying X-rays, Peter Kertesz for lending photographs of teeth, Ake Hedhammar in Sweden for help with translations and for finding photos of Horand, the first registered German Shepherd, and Ivan Gerger at the Waltham Centre of Pet Nutrition for providing advice on the German Shepherd's energy requirements.

PUBLISHER'S ACKNOWLEDGMENTS

Dorling Kindersley would like to thank photographer Tracy Morgan for her invaluable contribution to the book. Also special thanks to Tracy's photographic assistants: Sally Bergh-Roose, Stella Smyth-Carpenter, and Christina Hale. We are also very grateful to Patricia Holden White for her generous advice and help on photographic sessions. Thanks also to Karin Woodruff for the index, and to Sarah Kendall of The Company of Animals for supplying props. Finally, we would like to thank the following people for lending their dogs and/or for modelling:

Mitchell Andrews; Laurence Bard (Thunder); Wendy Bartlet; Roy and Maureen Beech (Rosie); Sally Bergh-Roose (Olderhill Abeth at Sarsway CDX UDX WDX TDX "Chaos", Sarsway Arak CDX UDX WD "Hudson", Sarsway Ardent CDX UD WD "Mallik", Yuarana Wild Joker "Rion", and Standahl Orie "Kes"); Allan and Marion Botchinsky (Theo); Ken, Chris, and Sheryl Brooks (Pepsi); Penny Carpanini (Tabathas Mirth "Mirth"); Connor and Judy Carroll (Oscar); Suzanne Collins (Karma); Bruce Fogle; Jill Fornary; David and Shantie Forrest (Lexter Jobey "Zack", Davantie Klamity Jane "Chloe", and the Davantie litter); Denise Frick (Bonnie Blue); Sarah and Victoria Goodwin; Christina Hale; Gillian Jane (Heelakeary Countess and her litter); Helen Lamb (Sabre); Sarah Lillicrapp; Hilary Lynette of the Conquell Dog Training Centre (Conquell Troila, Conquell Orrie, and Conquell Platz); Denise Murkett (Luke); Neil McAuliffe of Crown Protection Services Limited (Guinness, Murco, and Kelly); Tracy Morgan (Topkyri The Fire Dragon "Scorch"); Seán O'Connell; Valentine Olubodun; Mr. W. and Mrs. J. Petrie (Champion Bilnetts Dirty Harry, Bilnetts Lucky Charm, and the Bilnetts "N" litter); Ken and Anita Plaster of the Aylesbury German Shepherd Dog Training Club (Heelacullum Breen of Heelakeary "Bonnie", Heelakeary Arno "Dancer", and Heelakeary Baron "Lieka"); Anne Price (Flora and Marla); Nick Roeg (Anna); Jane Russell; Juette Shallow; Hester Small; Stella and Stephanie Smyth-Carpenter (Dinah).

PHOTOGRAPHIC CREDITS

Key: l=left, r=right, t=top, c=centre, a=above, b=below

All photography by Tracy Morgan except:
Animal Photography: (Sally Anne Thompson) 7cr, 17br, 73br, 74tl; **Jane Burton**: 56b; **Christopher Bradbury**: 64cr; **Mary Evans Picture Library**: 62cl, 74cr, 74bl; **Guide Dogs for the Blind Association**: 75tr; **The Image Bank**: (Lynn M. Stone) 6tl, (Joseph Van Os) 63br; **Impact Photos**: (Marilyn Greene) 75cl; **Microscopix Photo Library**: 52bl; **Rex Features**: (James Morgan) 72br, 72bl, 75bl, (Sipa Press) 75br; **Tim Ridley**: 4–5br, 7b, 8bl, 8br, 14cr, 14tl, 15c, 15tr, 22bl, 28–29, 33b, 42–43, 44bl, 44br, 44cr, 45bl, 45br, 46bl, 46c, 47br, 47tl, 49bl, 50b, 52t, 53, 56cr, 60b, 61bl, 61br, 61tl, 68cr, 70t; **Solitaire Photography**: 72ar, 73bl; **David Ward**: 7t, 18cl, 36bl, 37b; **Zefa Pictures**: 2.

ILLUSTRATIONS
Samantha Elmhurst: 53, 55, 65;
Sean Milne: 58–59;
Jane Pickering: 35;
Clive Spong: 11.